Free DVD **FREE** Free DVD

Essential Test Tips Video from Trivium Test Prep

Dear Customer,

Thank you for purchasing from Trivium Test Prep! Whether you're looking to join the military, get into college, or advance your career, we're honored to be a part of your journey.

To show our appreciation (and to help you relieve a little of that test-prep stress), we're offering a **FREE *RICA Essential Test Tips* Video** by Trivium Test Prep. Our video includes 35 test preparation strategies that will help keep you calm and collected before and during your big exam. All we ask is that you email us your feedback and describe your experience with our product. Amazing, awful, or just so-so: we want to hear what you have to say!

To receive your **FREE *RICA Essential Test Tips* Video**, please email us at 5star@ triviumtestprep.com. Include "Free 5 Star" in the subject line and the following information in your email:

1. The title of the product you purchased.

2. Your rating from 1 – 5 (with 5 being the best).

3. Your feedback about the product, including how our materials helped you meet your goals and ways in which we can improve our products.

4. Your full name and shipping address so we can send your **FREE *RICA Essential Test Tips* Video**.

If you have any questions or concerns please feel free to contact us directly at 5star@triviumtestprep.com.

Thank you, and good luck with your studies!

RICA Test Prep Book 2024-2025

Study Guide and 2 Practice Exams for the California Reading Instruction Competence Assessment

Eric Canizales

TABLE OF CONTENTS

Introduction to the RICA

Congratulations on choosing to take the Reading Instruction Competence Assessment (RICA)! By purchasing this book, you've taken the first step toward gaining the required credentials to become a multiple-subject teacher or education specialist (special education) in the state of California.

This guide will provide you with a detailed overview of the RICA, so you will know exactly what to expect on test day. We'll take you through all of the concepts covered on the exam and give you the opportunity to test your knowledge with practice questions. Even if it's been a while since you last took a major exam, don't worry; we'll make sure you're more than ready!

What is the RICA?

The Reading Instruction Competence Assessment (RICA) was developed by Evaluation Systems in partnership with the California Commission on Teacher Credentialing (CTC) to satisfy requirements set forth by Education Code Section 44283. The goal of the RICA is to evaluate the skills, knowledge, and abilities of multiple-subject or special education teacher candidates in the state of California as they relate to reading instruction.

What's on the RICA?

Candidates have the option of taking the written, computer-based exam at a testing center, or they may submit a series of videos if choosing to take the video performance assessment.

Computer-Based Test (Written Exam)

The computer-based exam consists of three subtests. The subtests may be taken together or individually. Each subtest contains multiple-choice and constructed-response portions, and the number of questions varies between subtests. The content of the subtests is based on numerous competencies (see https://www.ctcexams.nesinc.com/content/docs/RC_content_specs.pdf), which are divided into five domains.

What's on the Reading Instruction Competence Assessment (RICA)?	
Subtest I	
Domain 2(Word Analysis)	• 27 multiple-choice
	• 1 constructed-response (150 – 300 words)
Domain 3 (Fluency)	• 8 multiple-choice
	• 1 constructed-response (75 – 125 words)
Time Allowed	75 minutes
Subtest II	
Domain 4 (Vocabulary, Academic Language, Background Knowledge)	• 19 multiple-choice
	• 1 constructed-response (75 – 125 words)

What's on the Reading Instruction Competence Assessment (RICA)?		
Domain 5 (Comprehension)	▪ 16 (multiple-choice) ▪ 1 constructed-response (150 – 300 words)	
Time Allowed	75 minutes	
Subtest III		
Domain 1 (Planning, Organizing, Managing Reading Instruction Based on Ongoing Assessment)	▪ 25 multiple-choice ▪ 1 constructed-response (300 – 600 words)	
Time Allowed	90 minutes	

The domains referenced in each subtest are associated with your understanding of the following competencies:

Subtest I - Domain 2 (Word Analysis)

- how phonological and phonemic awareness each play roles in reading development and how students' phonological and phonemic awareness skills can be developed **(Competency 3)**
- how concepts about print, letter recognition, and the alphabetic principle play roles in reading development and ways in which students' knowledge and skills in these areas can be developed **(Competency 4)**
- critical terminology and concepts involved in phonics instruction; the role of phonics and sight words in reading development **(Competency 5)**
- how students' knowledge of phonics, skills, and recognition of sight words can be developed to promote accurate word analysis resulting in automaticity in word recognition and contributing to spelling development **(Competency 6)**
- syllabic analysis, structural analysis, orthographic knowledge, and the roles they play in reading development; ways to develop students' knowledge and skills in these areas to promote accurate word analysis that results in automaticity in word recognition and contributes to spelling development **(Competency 7)**

Subtest I – Domain 3 (Fluency)

- fluency and its role in reading development; factors that affect fluency development in students **(Competency 8)**
- how to promote fluency development in students **(Competency 9)**

Subtest II – Domain 4 (Vocabulary, Background Knowledge, Language Acquisition)

- vocabulary, academic language, background knowledge, and the roles these each play in reading development; factors affecting the development of vocabulary, academic language, and background knowledge in students **(Competency 10)**
- how to promote the development of vocabulary, academic language, and background knowledge in students **(Competency 11)**

1. Foundations of Language

Subtest II – Domain 5 (Comprehension)

- the different comprehension types (literal, inferential, and evaluative); factors that affect students' reading comprehension **(Competency 12)**
- how to facilitate reading comprehension through instruction aimed at preparing students for reading tasks; scaffolding students and preparing them to answer questions about what they have read **(Competency 13)**
- how to promote students' comprehension and analysis of narrative/literary texts; developing literary response skills in students **(Competency 14)**
- how to promote students' comprehension of informational and expository texts and developing students' study and research skills **(Competency 15)**

Subtest III – Domain 1 (Planning, Organizing, Managing Reading Instruction Based on Ongoing Assessment)

- how to plan, organize, and manage standards-based reading instruction **(Competency 1)**
- the purposes of reading assessments and best practices as concerns standards-based, entry-level assessment, summative assessment, and student progress monitoring **(Competency 2)**

Video Performance Assessment

Instead of sitting for the computer-based exam, candidates have the option of submitting videos that show how they teach students to read. The assessment is based on your performance in a classroom setting. Candidates who choose this option must submit **three videos** that each contain the following components:

- an instructional context form (includes lesson plans and information about students)
- a 10-minute video/recording (must show candidate demonstrating reading instruction)
- a reflection form (includes a self-appraisal with thoughts about using different instructional methods)

Official templates exist that must accompany each video; these can be found by visiting https://www.ctcexams.nesinc.com and choosing the "RICA Video Performance Assessment Option." The three required videos and their corresponding templates are broken down as follows:

1. whole-class instruction
2. small-group instruction
3. individual instruction

The videos must demonstrate the candidate's ability to carry out the competencies as described above. Specific details can be found in the CTC's *Video Performance Assessment Guide* (https://www.ctcexams.nesinc.com/Content/Docs/RICA_Video_AssessmentGuide.pdf).

What is the Passing Score on the RICA?

Computer-Based Test (Written Exam)

A minimum score of 220 *per subtest* is required to pass the RICA. Test results are typically available within three weeks from the date on which you take the exam.

Video Performance Assessment

A minimum score of 220 *per video* is required to pass the RICA. Your test score will typically be available about three weeks after the videos have been submitted.

How is the RICA Administered?

The computer-based test (written exam) is offered at Pearson Vue test sites across the nation. Visit https://home.pearsonvue.com/ to determine which test center location works best for you. Candidates taking the computer-based test (written exam) also have the option of taking the exam at home through online proctoring.

Whether taking the computer-based exam or submitting materials for the video performance assessment, all fees must be paid in full beforehand. Fees are broken down as follows:

- $57 per subtest (computer-based exam)
- $171 (video performance assessment)

Eligible candidates may be able to have their test fees waived. Visit https://www.ctcexams.nesinc.com for more information.

About Cirrus Test Prep

Cirrus Test Prep study guides are designed by current and former educators and tailored to meet your needs as an incoming educator. Our guides offer all of the resources necessary to help you pass teacher certification tests across the nation.

Cirrus clouds are graceful, wispy clouds characterized by their high altitude. Just like cirrus clouds, Cirrus Test Prep's goal is to help educators "aim high" when it comes to obtaining their teacher certifications and entering the classroom.

About This Guide

This guide will help you master the most important test topics and develop critical test-taking skills. We have built features into our books to prepare you for your exam and increase your score. Along with a detailed summary of the test's format and content, we offer an in-depth overview of the content knowledge required to pass the test. Our sidebars provide interesting information, highlight key ideas, and review content so that you can solidify your understanding of the exam's concepts. Test your knowledge with sample questions and detailed answer explanations in the text that help you think through the problems on the exam and practice questions that reflect the content and format of the RICA. We're pleased you've chosen Cirrus to be a part of your professional journey!

1. Foundations of Language

The Five Domains of Effective Reading Instruction

The Reading Instruction Competence Assessment (RICA) aims to ensure that entry-level teachers in the state of California can deliver effective, assessment-based reading instruction to their students. To do this, teachers must

- have a deep understanding of reading standards by grade level (as set by the state of California),
- ensure that the reading curriculum in their classrooms is comprehensive yet balanced, and
- be mindful of varying student needs in the classroom.

The RICA exam will evaluate candidates' knowledge and skills—known as *competencies*—as they pertain to effective reading instruction. These competencies are organized within five domains as described in Table 1.1.

Table 1.1. RICA Domains and Associated Competencies	
Domain 1	
Description	**Associated Competencies**
<ul><li>planning</li><li>organizing</li><li>managing reading instruction (based on ongoing assessments)</li></ul>	planning, organizing, and managing standards-based reading instruction; the goals of reading assessments; standards-based and entry-level assessments and best practices; summative assessments; monitoring student progress
Domain 2	
Description	**Associated Competencies**
<ul><li>analysis of words</li></ul>	reading development, the role of phonological and phonemic awareness, and developing these skills in students; concepts of print, letter recognition and their roles in learning how to read; phonics terminology and sight words; phonics to teach word analysis and recognition; syllable and spelling development
Domain 3	
Description	**Associated Competencies**
<ul><li>fluency</li></ul>	the role of fluency in reading; promoting reading fluency in students
Domain 4	
Description	**Associated Competencies**
<ul><li>vocabulary</li><li>academic language</li></ul>	academic language, vocabulary, and background knowledge and their roles in reading development and how to promote students' development of these

Table 1.1. RICA Domains and Associated Competencies	
Domain 1	
Description	**Associated Competencies**
• background knowledge	
Domain 5	
Description	**Associated Competencies**
• comprehension	literal, inferential, and evaluative comprehension as they affect overall reading comprehension; an understanding of how to instruct and prepare students to read for comprehension, including scaffolding

In order to properly teach students how to read, read for comprehension, and respond to questions about what they have read, teachers need to have an in-depth understanding of the foundations of language, which is the focus of this chapter.

Practice Question

1) Which of the following is NOT needed in order for teachers to deliver effective, assessment-based reading instruction to their students?

    A. having a deep understanding of reading standards by grade level

    B. personal experience dealing with the challenges of reading instruction

    C. ensuring that the reading curriculum in classrooms is comprehensive and balanced

    D. being mindful of varying student needs in the classroom

Stages of Literacy Development

To achieve full **literacy**, or the ability to read and write, children often go through stages. Before children begin to sound out words, they are in an **emergent literacy** stage. This first stage typically lasts from preschool to early kindergarten. During the emergent literacy phase, children are able to recognize **environmental print**, or words in their surroundings, such as the word *STOP* on a red stop sign. They may also know the letters and even some letter sounds. Children then develop **alphabetic fluency**, where they begin to apply phonics skills, decode basic words, and read orally word-by-word. This second stage signals the learning-to-read stage and often begins in late kindergarten and lasts through first grade.

In the third stage of literacy development, often referred to as the **transitional stage**, students are less reliant on adult help for unknown words and instead begin to apply strategies on their own. In this stage, children begin comprehending the whole text instead of reading word-by-word. This stage often occurs during second grade.

After the transitional stage, students enter the **intermediate stage**. This fourth stage marks the movement from learning to read to reading to learn. Many experts believe students must be reading to learn by the end of third grade in order to have the best opportunity for learning in the years that follow. In the

intermediate stage, students begin to read longer texts, learn vocabulary, and consider perspectives in the texts they encounter.

In the fifth and final stage of literacy learning, **advanced reading**, students are fully fluent and can read and write a variety of complex texts. The timing of the advanced reading stage may vary but it often emerges between the ages of eleven and fourteen.

Practice Question

2) When should students IDEALLY begin reading to learn instead of learning to read?
   A. first grade
   B. second grade
   C. third grade
   D. fourth grade

Foundations of Language

Human Language

Human language varies among cultures throughout the world, but all languages share some similarities:

- All languages are learned by human babies at roughly the same time, regardless of location.

- All languages have basic rules—**grammar**—that specify how words should be put together.

- Languages from anywhere in the world have ways for people to communicate when in time actions occur; the ways in which these times are indicated (e.g., verb conjugation, word endings, separate words) vary widely.

- All languages have formal, casual, and slang forms as well as various dialects and accents.

  o Dialects and accents may be particular to certain geographic locations or groups.

  o In contrast to a dialects are **idiolects**, which are particular language forms or structures used solely by one individual.

Furthermore, all languages are rooted in the context of their use. **Pragmatics** is the study of language within its context. Language can also be studied in terms of the following:

- **phonology** (the organization of sounds)

- **morphology** (the study of words and their parts)

- **syntax** (how words combine to form groups, such as phrases, clauses, and sentences)

- **semantics** (the study of what words mean or to what they refer)

Practice Question

3) Which statement BEST describes how all languages are similar?
   A.   They use verb conjugation.
   B.   They are learned at roughly the same time.
   C.   They are spoken in a single accent.
   D.   They use words to show when in time actions occur.

Morphology

Morphology is the study of words and their parts, which are known as **morphemes**. Morphemes come in various types and are discussed in detail in Chapter 2. Briefly, morphemes can be broken down as follows:

- **Free morphemes** are words on their own (*help, go, big*).
- **Bound morphemes** must be added to another morpheme (e.g., *-ly, -ing, un-*).
- **Derivational morphemes** are affixes (prefixes and suffixes) that, when added to another word, create a new word.
- **Inflectional morphemes** simply denote a plural or tense but do not make an entirely new word or change the word to a new part of speech.

Morphemes are distinct from syllables in that syllabication refers to patterns and word divisions related to pronunciation while morphemes refer to patterns based on meaning. Often syllabication is a strategy for sounding out words orally while morphemic analysis is a spelling or vocabulary strategy

With roots and affixes, or **derivational morphemes**, new words are formed. For example, *cent* is a Latin root meaning "one hundred." **Affixes** are added to words or roots to change their meanings. There are two types of affixes: prefixes and suffixes. A **prefix** is added to the beginning of a word and usually changes its meaning. For example, the prefix *per-* can be added to the term *cent* to make the word *percent*, effectively changing the meaning to "one part in a hundred." A suffix, which is added to the end of a word, can also change a word's meaning as well as help readers determine a word's grammatical information. For example, the suffix *–ury* can be added to the term *cent* to make the word *century*, effectively changing the meaning to "a period of one hundred years."

Table 1.2. Common Roots with Affixes		
Root	**Definition**	**Example**
ast(er)	star	asteroid, astronomy
audi	hear	audience, audible
auto	self	automatic, autograph
bene	good	beneficent, benign
bio	life	biology, biorhythm

Table 1.2. Common Roots with Affixes

Root	Definition	Example
cap	take	capture
ced	yield	secede
chrono	time	chronometer, chronic
corp	body	corporeal
crac/crat	rule	autocrat
demo	people	democracy
dict	say	dictionary, dictation
duc	lead/make	ductile, produce
gen	give birth	generation, genetics
geo	Earth	geography, geometry
grad	step	graduate
graph	write	graphical, autograph
ject	throw	eject
jur/jus	law	justice, jurisdiction
log or logue	thought	logic, logarithm
luc	light	lucidity
man	hand	manual
mand	order	remand
mis	send	transmission
mono	one	monotone
omni	all	omnivore
path	feel	pathology
phil	love	philanthropy

Table 1.2. Common Roots with Affixes		
Root	**Definition**	**Example**
phon	sound	phonograph
port	carry	export
qui	rest	quiet
scrib or script	write	scribe, transcript
sense or sent	feel	sentiment
tele	far away	telephone
terr	the earth	terrace
uni	single	unicode
vac	empty	vacant
vid	see	video
vis	see	vision

Did You Know?

English words that come from French or German terms often originate from Latin words. The great majority of English words therefore have true Greek or Latin origins.

Related to morphology is **etymology**, which is the study of the history or origin of words. It often focuses on tracing the root word back to its origin and meaning.

Practice Questions

4) Use roots and affixes to determine the meaning of the term *monograph*.

    A. a mathematical concept

    B. a written study of a single subject

    C. an illness caused by a virus

    D. a boring piece of art

5) Use roots and affixes to determine the meaning of the term *polyglot*.

    A. a person who speaks many languages

    B. a person who loves to travel

    C. a person who is extremely intelligent

    D. a person who is unafraid of new places

English Language Development and Acquisition

Language acquisition is the process through which humans develop the ability to understand and create words and sentences in order to communicate. Many experts believe that children have an innate ability to acquire **oral language** from their environments. Even before babies can speak, they cry and coo in reaction to environmental stimuli or to communicate their needs. They recognize basic variants in the speech patterns of those around them, such as **articulation**, which is defined as the distinct sounds of speech; they can also identify contrasts when exposed to new languages. With this awareness, cooing and crying quickly turn into **babbling**, the first stage of language acquisition. This stage generally lasts from six months to around twelve months. In this stage, infants make a variety of sounds but may begin to focus on sounds for which they receive positive reinforcement. For example, babbles such as *baba* and *yaya* tend to garner praise and excitement from parents, so these may be repeated until the coveted *mama* or *dada* is produced.

Children start using first words—usually nouns—around age one, though this varies from child to child. During this single-word, or **holophrastic stage**, solitary words are generally used to express entire ideas. For example, "Toy!" may mean "Give me the toy." After a few months, this shifts to two-word utterances, such as "Mommy go" or "David bad." The **two-word stage** may last through early toddlerhood but generally gives rise to the **telegraphic phase** of oral language development at around age two and

> **Did You Know?**
>
> Ninety-five percent of all babbling by babies throughout the world is composed of only twelve consonants: *p, b, t, d, k, g, m, n, s, h, w, j.*

a half. In this stage, speech patterns become more advanced, though sometimes prepositions, articles, and other short words are missing. Telegraphic speech includes phrases such as "See plane go!" and "There go teacher." This stage persists until children are mostly fluent in the home language, generally at age three or four.

Practice Question

6) A young child utters "go" to ask to go to the playground. In which stage of language development is this child?

- A. babbling
- B. two-word stage
- C. telegraphic phase
- D. holophrastic stage

English Language Development and Acquisition for Non-Native Speakers

Not all students learn English as their first language. Some students may have **limited English proficiency**, which is a limited ability to read, speak, write, or understand English because it is not one's primary language.

Since early childhood is when students best learn new languages, many schools have programs designed to develop **dual language learners**, which are defined as those who are learning two languages simultaneously. This may take the form of a language immersion program where young children who speak English are placed in an environment where another language is spoken for part or most of the day. These programs are generally made up of students with a monolingual English background and students with some proficiency in a second language, with the goal of having students develop both languages through classroom instruction and social interaction with their peers.

Dual language programs can also take another form wherein students who speak only English at home are placed in a completely immersive environment to quickly become proficient in a second language. These programs have become very popular in many large cities as the need for a workforce that is fluent in more than one language continues to grow.

Children whose home languages are not English will be dual language learners in most typical, majority-English education programs. These young children, who are still developing skills in their home languages as part of the natural arc of child development, will also be developing skills in a second language. Teachers working with dual language learners must promote English language skills while supporting the ongoing development of the children's home languages. This **bilingualism**, or the ability to fluently speak two languages, is a huge benefit to the child and should therefore be nurtured. Children who develop two or more languages simultaneously have been found to have advantages in social-emotional development, early language and literacy, and overall cognitive development.

These students should also be encouraged to pursue **biliteracy**, or the ability to proficiently read and write in two languages. While language immersion programs will likely offer this component explicitly, all teachers can encourage students and families to read and write in both English and their home languages as appropriate so as to develop these proficiencies. Some districts and schools offer classroom curriculum resources in languages other than English to encourage this, and many educational publishers and technology companies offer resources in commonly spoken second languages, such as Spanish. Above all, when there are students who are learning English, teachers should not push them to discard or stop developing their heritage languages.

Children who are learning two languages may engage in **code-switching**, or alternating between two languages or dialects. Code-switching occurs most often in children when they begin a sentence in one language but complete it in another. This is a somewhat remarkable thing, and it shows that these children are maintaining grammatical rules in both languages. Code-switching is natural, normal, and expected, and it is no cause for concern. Rather than chiding students for code-switching, teachers should use these opportunities to expand students' vocabulary and knowledge in both languages, dependent, of course, on the teacher's proficiency in the children's native languages. Constantly correcting students for code-switching undermines their overall development and does not validate their need to communicate.

Students in the primary grades who have already developed fluency in their home languages but who have limited English proficiency are not considered dual language learners but rather **English language learners (ELLs)**, which are defined as students who need specialized instruction in English and other academic subject areas due to a lack of English proficiency. Instruction for these students will also vary considerably based on the program; however, most research suggests that best practices include helping students obtain English proficiency quickly while providing appropriate support and differentiation so that students can continue learning across content areas. It is important for teachers, especially of young students who may feel nervous in a new environment at first, to make English language learners feel comfortable in the classroom. Teachers can do that through strategies such as using visuals and predictable routines and by not forcing students to speak until they are ready.

Some students will go through a **silent period** where they may not speak much, and this is normal when learning a new language. Students may also be reluctant to practice newly acquired English language skills for fear of making mistakes, so teachers should make sure the classroom is a safe space where all attempts to use the new language are validated and praised.

Helpful Hint:
Interlanguage effects can be thought of as rules that may or may not always be true and that may have been learned when trying to acquire a second language. (E.g., Spanish language learners are often taught that nouns ending in *–o* are masculine and nouns ending in *–a* are feminine. While a helpful rule, there are exceptions: the word *el mapa* is a masculine noun that ends with *–a*, for example.

The acquisition of a second language should not always be viewed as a linear progression. When students acquire a second language, they also develop what is known as an **interlanguage**, or a system of rules for the use of the new language. Interlanguage can be based on the rules of the student's first language or the rules of both the first and new languages. It can even be based on features of neither language. **Interlanguage effects** can therefore sometimes work against second-language development if based on erroneous assumptions or nonexistent patterns.

Five **stages of language acquisition** have been identified for students learning a second language (see Table 1.3.). These stages are defined as preproduction, early production, speech emergence, intermediate fluency, and advanced fluency and correlate to five **levels of language proficiency**:

- L1 (entering)
- L2 (beginning)
- L3 (developing)
- L4 (expanding)

- L5 (bridging)

Table 1.3. Stages of Second-Language Acquisition	
Stage	**Characteristics**
Preproduction	This stage is also known as the silent period. Though learners in this stage may have close to 500 words in their receptive vocabularies, they refrain from speaking but will listen and may copy words down. They can respond to visual cues (i.e., pictures and gestures) and communicate their comprehension; however, students will sometimes just repeat what they have heard—a process known as parroting. Parroting aids students in adding to their receptive vocabularies, but it should not be mistaken for producing language.
Early production	In this stage, learners have achieved 1,000-word receptive and active vocabularies. They now produce single-word and two- to three-word phrases and can respond to questions and statements. Many learners in this stage enjoy engaging in musical games or word plays that help them memorize language chunks that they can use later.
Speech emergence	English language learners have a vocabulary of about 3,000 words by the time they reach this stage of second-language acquisition. They are able to chunk simple words and phrases into sentences that may or may not be grammatically correct. They respond to modeling of correct responses better than direct correction. At this stage, learners are also more likely to participate in conversations with native speakers since they are gaining confidence in their language skills. These learners can understand simple readings when reinforced by graphics or pictures and can complete some content work with support.
Intermediate fluency	By the intermediate fluency stage, second-language learners have acquired a vocabulary of about 6,000 words. They are able to speak in more complex sentences and catch and correct many of their errors. They are also willing to ask questions to clarify what they do not understand. Learners at this stage may sound fluent, but they have large gaps in their vocabulary as well as in their grammatical and syntactical understanding of the language. They are often comfortable speaking in group conversations that avoid heavy academic language.

Table 1.3. Stages of Second-Language Acquisition	
Stage	**Characteristics**
Advanced Fluency	Second-language learners who reach advanced fluency have achieved cognitive language proficiency in their learned language. They demonstrate near-native ability and use complex, multi phrase, and clause sentences to convey their ideas. Though accents are still detectable and idiomatic expressions are sometimes used incorrectly, the language learner has essentially become fluent.

Practice Question

7) Marlin enjoys participating in class discussions with his peers and even initiates them occasionally. Though he sometimes makes errors in his speech, he is able to self-correct and often repeats the correct phrasing back to himself. In which stage of second-language acquisition might Marlin be?

- A. preproduction
- B. early production
- C. speech emergence
- D. intermediate fluency

Language Structure and Literacy Foundations

Humans learn language in predictable patterns that often combine speaking, reading, and writing. Such language development typically begins with an understanding of sounds.

Phonological awareness is an understanding of how sounds, syllables, words, and word parts can be orally manipulated to break apart words, make new words, and create rhymes. It is an important foundational skill for learning to read and literacy development. **Phonemic awareness** is a type of phonological awareness that focuses on the sounds in a language. It is an understanding of how each small unit of sound, or **phoneme**, forms the language by creating differences in the meanings of words. For example, the phonemes /m/ and /s/ determine the differences in meaning between the words mat and sat.

Producing and creating oral rhymes	**Singing songs with alliteration**	**Clapping and other hand movements** (e.g., clapping for onsets and rimes in words, clapping for each word in a sentence)	**Learning alphabet songs**
Listening for and identifying the sounds at the beginning, middle, and end of CVC words	**Orally blending, segmenting, and manipulating phonemes in words**	**Sorting pictures according to beginning or ending sound**	**Using finger spelling,** which is a form of sign language that uses the hands to represent letters

Figure 1.1. Phonological Awareness Strategies

There are forty-four different phonemes in the English language. These include letter combinations, such as consonant diagraphs (e.g., /sh/) and vowel diphthongs (e.g., /oi/) where the letters work together to produce one sound. Teachers build phonemic awareness in their students by using a variety of techniques, such as phoneme blending, phoneme segmentation, phoneme substitution, and phoneme deletion.

Phoneme blending is combining phonemes to make a word; for example, /m/ /a/ /t/ combines to form the word *mat*. **Phoneme segmentation** is separating phonemes into words. For example, separating the sounds in the word *mat* isolates the phonemes */m/ /a/ /t/*.

Building phonemic awareness in students is the latter part of a developmental sequence that contributes to a strong foundation in phonological awareness. Prior to focusing on phonemic awareness, teachers build phonological awareness with exercises that task students with orally manipulating the phonological units of spoken **syllables**. These phonological units are defined as onsets and rimes and can be blended, substituted, segmented, and deleted just like phonemes. The **onset** of a syllable is the beginning consonant or consonant blend. The **rime** includes the syllable's vowel and its remaining consonants. For example, in the word *block*, the consonant blend /bl/ is the onset, and the remainder of the word –*ock* is the rime.

> **Helpful Hint:**
>
> Remember that onsets are the first part of the word, or the first "button" readers see—the "ON" button. Rimes are the parts of the word that rhyme such as c-*at*, h-*at*, b-*at*, and so on.

Practice Question

8) What is the focus of phonemic awareness?

    A. the meaning of language

    B. the rhythm and patterns of language

    C. the sounds in a language

    D. avoiding repetition of phonemes in written text

The Alphabetic Principle

The **alphabetic principle** presumes an understanding that words are made up of written letters or symbols that represent spoken sounds. In order to procced with more advanced reading concepts, children must first have a firm grasp of letter sounds. Students should be given many opportunities to develop **letter-sound correspondence**, or the recognition and association of a letter with its sound.

There is no firm rule on the pace at which the letter sounds should be mastered. Most experts agree that high-frequency letters should be introduced first, as well as those that allow children to sound out short words quickly. It is sometimes easier for children to master simple sounds like /t/ and /s/ before tackling more challenging or confusing sounds like /b/, /d/, and /i/.

Did You Know?

Most strategies for introducing students to the letter sounds draw on **high-frequency letter-sound correspondence**, whereby the most frequent and useful letter sounds are taught first. This allows students to begin reading as soon as possible without having to master each letter sound.

Regardless of how teachers practice the alphabetic principle (e.g., a letter of the week or teaching the letters in succession), they should recognize that repetition is key. Students should have many opportunities to practice each letter and sound. Letter sounds should first be taught explicitly and in isolation from one another. From there, students can practice saying the sounds of letters and sounding out simple words in context. The following list describes strategies for teaching the alphabetic principle and letter-sound correspondence:

- Begin instruction with lowercase letters, as these are the primary letters used in forming words.
- Avoid overemphasis of letter *names* and focus primarily on letter *sounds*. Students do not need to know letter names to learn to read, and some students may be confused by the distinction between the letter name and the letter sound.
- Teach easy consonants first, followed by easy vowel sounds, introducing a new sound every two or three days.
- Teach the most common sound a letter makes first. For example, the letter *g* should be associated with the sound it makes in *grass* before associating it with the sound it makes in *rage*.
- Teach letters that look similar and/or have somewhat similar sounds (e.g., /b/ and /d/ or /m/ and /n/) separately and to limit confusion.
- Model the correct pronunciation when teaching letter sounds, introducing continuous sounds (*f, l, m, n, r, s, v, w, y,* and *z*) before stop sounds (*b, c, d, g, j, k, p, q, t*). Stop sounds require control to pronounce correctly (/b/ for *b* versus "buh" for *b*).

- Teach short vowel sounds before long vowel sounds. This is practical and allows young readers to begin to sound out short consonant-vowel-consonant (CVC) words like *dig* and *run*.

The following activities promote letter-sound correspondence:

- Use letter-sound charts or letter-sound flashcards with or without picture cues with individual students, small groups, or the entire class. The "I say, you say, we say" method can be used effectively with these tools.
- Create alphabet boards or even a computer keyboard with lowercase letters taped over the appropriate keys for instructional or assessment activities. As the teacher says a sound, students can point to the letter, type it, or move a tile over it.
- Have students trace or form lowercase letters with pens, pencils, or in sand or shaving cream while saying the sound that each letter makes. This can develop fine motor skills and reinforce letter-sound correspondence.
- Have students sort items into groups or piles based on initial letter sound. For example, students could place all the toy animals or pictures of animals with a /c/ sound in one group or pile.
- Use alphabet picture books for guided storybook reading, and stop during reading to reinforce and practice letter sounds. *Chicka Chicka Boom Boom* by Bill Martin Jr. and John Archambault and *Eating the Alphabet* by Lois Ehlert are popular choices.
- Have students draw a line around, color in, or circle all items on the page that begin with a given letter sound.

> **Did You Know?**
>
> "The ABC song" was copyrighted in 1835 but is actually an adaptation of a Mozart melody.

Practice Question

9) Which activity is MOST appropriate for students to practice onsets and the alphabetic principle?

    A. having them sort toy animals into tubs based on the initial letter sound of the animal's name

    B. asking them to help clap out the syllables in a student's name

    C. asking them to point to a sentence on a page

    D. having them remove a sound from a word and say the new word

Answer Key

1) B: While having firsthand experience with reading instruction challenges could prove helpful, it is not necessary in order to deliver effective, assessment-based reading instruction to students.

2) C: Experts concur that by the end of third grade, students should make the shift from the transitional stage to the intermediate stage of literacy development.

3) B: All languages are learned by human babies at roughly the same time.

4) B: The prefix *mono–* means "one," and the root word *graph* means "written," so a monograph is a written document about one subject.

5) A: The prefix *poly–* means "many," and the suffix *–glot* means "in a language or tongue." Therefore, the sentence is explaining that the sister speaks many languages.

6) D: In the holophrastic stage, children use one word to denote a broader desire or meaning. This is the stage after babbling.

7) D: Marlin's interest in conversation and his ability to self-correct indicate that he is moving towards advanced fluency and has reached the intermediate stage.

8) C: Phonemic awareness is a type of phonological awareness that focuses on the sounds in a language. It is an understanding of how each small unit of sound (i.e., phoneme) forms the language by creating differences in the meanings of words.

9) A: This sorting exercise helps students identify both letter sounds and the initial sounds of words.

2. Phonics and Spelling

Print Awareness

Print awareness involves a basic understanding of the nature of reading: English is read from left to right and top to bottom, and words are read on a page. Very young children without solid print awareness may believe that meaning is gleaned from pictures on a page rather than words. Some younger children may understand that books convey meaning but may not quite know how. Teachers may see these children model reading a book upside down.

Concepts of print are the principles that must be mastered before learning to read and are key to print awareness. These principles include knowledge and identification of a word, letter, and sentence; knowledge of the many uses of print; and knowledge of the overarching structure of a book or story (title, beginning, middle, end).

Many young students have some print awareness through environmental print. **Environmental print** describes the words children see regularly in their environment, like product names, street signs, business names, and menus at restaurants. Teachers can use popular environmental print, like the names and logos of popular children's products, stores, and restaurants, to encourage pre-readers to "read" these words.

Teachers should also consider using environmental print in each of their students' home languages in the classroom. For example, a teacher might label the door in English, Spanish, Thai, and Vietnamese. This builds confidence and familiarity and reinforces the idea that these words in languages other than English also have meaning.

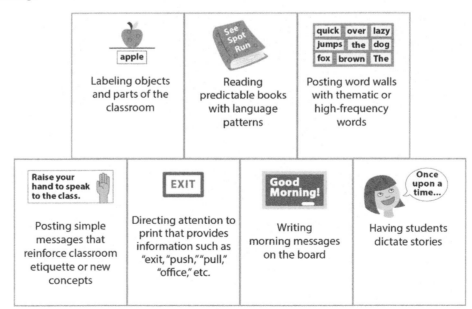

Figure 2.1. Concepts of Print Classroom Strategies

Teachers should also point to words (rather than pictures) on a page and instruct young students to do the same during storybook reading. This will reinforce concepts of print and help students develop print

awareness. Such practice will help even very young students begin to understand that, while both the pictures and words on the page contribute to the overall meaning, the part being read is the words—not the pictures.

Practice Question

1) Which activity will BEST help gauge a student's print awareness?

   A. asking him to recount story events

   B. asking her to point to a sentence

   C. asking him to write the letter *p*

   D. asking her what sound the letter *p* makes

Phonics and Phonics Instruction

Phonics

Phonics is an age-old strategy for helping students read by connecting written language to spoken language or by correlating certain sounds with certain letters or groups of letters. Letter-sound correspondence is a foundational skill for effective phonics instruction since most phonics strategies will require students to draw rapidly on this memory bank of letter sounds. Most strategies for introducing students to the letter sounds draw on **high-frequency letter-sound correspondence**, where the most frequent and useful letter sounds are taught first. This will allow students to begin reading as soon as possible without having to master each letter sound.

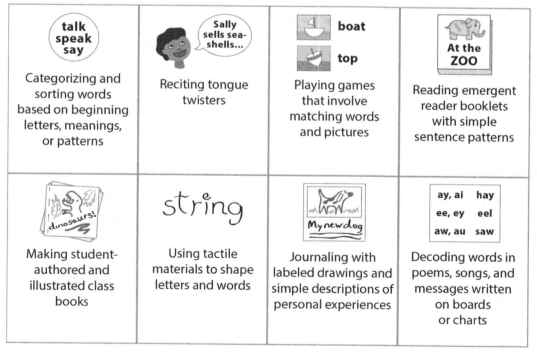

| talk speak say — Categorizing and sorting words based on beginning letters, meanings, or patterns | Sally sells sea-shells... — Reciting tongue twisters | boat / top — Playing games that involve matching words and pictures | At the ZOO — Reading emergent reader booklets with simple sentence patterns |
| dinosaurs! — Making student-authored and illustrated class books | string — Using tactile materials to shape letters and words | My new dog — Journaling with labeled drawings and simple descriptions of personal experiences | ay, ai hay / ee, ey eel / aw, au saw — Decoding words in poems, songs, and messages written on boards or charts |

Figure 2.2. Phonics Classroom Strategies

As part of phonics learning, students will learn that the English alphabet contains both **consonants** and **vowels** but that it also contains much more complex structures, such as consonant blends where two or more consonants make a single sound (e.g., /bl/ or /tr/).

Students will also require instruction in **graphemes**, or ways of recording sounds. Grapheme units can be single letters that makes a sound (e.g., /i/), or a sequence of letters that makes a sound (e.g., /ai/). A single sound can also be represented by multiple graphemes. For example, the long /a/ sound can be made by both the words _ray_ and _weigh_.

Part of helping students become strong decoders (discussed in the next section) is teaching certain patterns in the English language so that students can recognize these when they encounter unfamiliar words. One of these patterns involves syllables, which can be segmented into multisyllabic words, as described in Table 2.1.

Table 2.1. Syllable Patterns

Syllable Type	Description	Examples
Closed syllables	end in a consonant short vowel sound	hat hip-ster
Open syllables	end with a vowel long vowel sound	go lo-cate
Vowel-consonant-_e_ (VC_e_)	end with silent -_e_ long vowel sound	take ren-o-vate
Vowel teams	more than one vowel letter makes one sound	sea green-er
R-controlled syllables	vowel + _R_	stir in-jur-ious
Consonant-le (C-le)	consonant + le	ta-ble lit-tle

There are some syllable patterns that do not fall into any of these types such as -_ive_, -_ion_, -_age_, and -_ture_.

Syllable division patterns, as described in Table 2.2., can also help students decode and spell words.

Table 2.2. Syllable Division Patterns

Syllable Pattern	Description	Examples
vowel, consonant, consonant, vowel (VCCV)	The syllable division is between the two consonants; the accent is on the first or second syllable.	• in/sect • com/bine • in/sist
vowel, consonant, vowel (VCV)	The syllable division is before the consonant and the accent is on the first or second syllable.	• ro-bin • re/quest

Table 2.2. Syllable Division Patterns

Syllable Pattern	Description	Examples
		• u/nite
vowel, consonant, consonant, consonant, vowel (VCCCV)	The syllable division is after the first consonant and the accent is on the first or second syllable.	• sand/wich • hun/dred • ex/treme

Students may also benefit from learning about **vowel combinations** (digraphs and trigraphs), as seen in Table 2.3.

Table 2.3. Vowel Combinations (Digraphs and Trigraphs)

ai	ee	ign	olt
au	ea	ing	oll
ay	eu	oo	ou
aw	ew	oa	ow
augh	ei	oe	ue
all	ey	oi	ui
ald	eigh	oy	oll
alm	le	old	ou
alt	igh	olk	

Practice Question

2) How is decoding related to language patterns in English?

   A. Students must first know how to decode before they can recognize language patterns.

   B. Students can use the patterns they recognize to help them decode unfamiliar words.

   C. They are taught simultaneously.

   D. They are not related.

Morphemes and Morphology

Students should also learn to analyze the structure of word parts, known as **morphemes**. Morphemes come in various types, as described in Table 2.4.

Table 2.4. Types of Morphemes		
Type	**Definition**	**Examples**
Free morphemes	• words used on their own	*help, go, big*
Bound morphemes	• those which must be added to another morpheme	*-ly, -ing, un-*
Derivational morphemes	• affixes (prefixes and suffixes) that, when added to another word, create a new word • essential building blocks of the English language • **added to** base words in English or **roots** often derived from Latin or Greek	prefixes: *un-, re-, pre-* suffixes: *-able, -ive, -ion*
Inflectional morphemes	• denote a plural or tense but do not make an entirely new word or change the word to a new part of speech	*-s, -ed, -ing* NOTE: Knowing the most common inflectional morphemes and their spellings can help young readers and writers.

Practice Question

3) Which of the following is BOTH a derivational morpheme and a bound morpheme?

    A. -ed

    B. -ion

    C. -s

    D. un-

Phonics Instruction and Decoding

Once students have solid foundations in phonological awareness, they are ready to begin phonics instruction. **Phonics** is the study of the relationship between the spoken sounds in words and the printed letters that correspond to those sounds, or **letter-sound correspondence, sometimes referred to as sound-symbol correspondence**. In explicit phonics instruction, letters and their corresponding sounds are first taught in isolation and then blended into words; finally, they are applied to decodable text.

Phonics instruction draws on the strategy of **decoding**, or the ability to pronounce the sounds of written words orally and glean meaning. Because of its focus on the specific sound structures of words, phonics instruction tends to involve more explicit, direct instruction and is not without critics, who believe it overemphasizes the mechanics of reading while sacrificing the enjoyment. Most classrooms today, however, employ a combination approach that balances inquiry-based student learning and allows for the open exploration of high-interest literacy games and activities, with more direct phonics instruction.

Helpful Hint:

There are four types of phonics instruction: synthetic phonics instruction (explicit, direct instruction of phonemes and graphemes); analytic phonics instruction (focuses on onset and rime); analogy phonics instruction (focuses on word families); and embedded phonics instruction (teaches phonics via actual books).

Research has identified explicit, systematic phonics instruction as being highly effective.

Many words are **decodable**, meaning they follow basic principles of phonics. Students should be able to sound these words out once they master basic structural deviations, like long vowel sounds with a word ending in –*e*, and various digraphs, where two letters make a single sound such as /th/ and /ay/.

Other words are **non-decodable**, meaning they deviate from the standard rules of phonics. Typically, these words must simply be memorized through frequent exposure. These words must be presented to students with great frequency so they can be memorized. Such words must become **sight words**, or words that require no decoding because they are instantly recognized and read automatically.

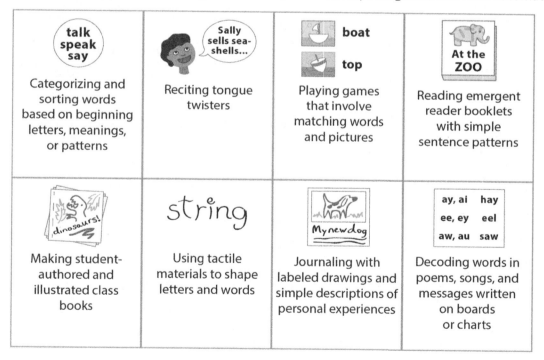

Figure 2.3. Phonics Strategies

Initially, the most common sounds for each letter and **high-frequency** letter-sound correspondences, or those that occur most often in the English language, are introduced. In order to assist students who are beginning to read simple vowel-consonant (VC), vowel-consonant-consonant (VCC), consonant-vowel-consonant-consonant (CVCC), and consonant-vowel-consonant (CVC) words early on, a few short vowel

sounds are introduced as well. Letters with names that bear a strong relationship to their sounds are introduced before letters that do not. For example, the sound of the letter *s* can be heard at the end of its name.

Phonics instruction progresses from simple to more complex letter-sound correspondences and sounds/spellings (or the spellings of words based on letter-sound correspondences). Short-vowel sound spellings are introduced before long-vowel sound/spellings, and letters that are similar in appearance (e.g., *b* and *d*) or sound (e.g., /m/ and /n/) are taught separately along the instructional continuum. As students move through kindergarten and the primary grades, they progress from decoding two- or three-phoneme words with letters representing their most common sounds to longer words and more complex sound/spelling patterns.

Table 2.5. Phoneme Chart

Phoneme	Example	Phoneme	Example	Phoneme	Example
Consonants		*Vowels*		*R-Controlled Vowels*	
/b/	bat	/a/	lap	/ã/	hair
/d/	dog	/ā/	late	/ä/	art
/f/	fish	/e/	bet	/û/	dirt
/g/	goat	/ē/	see	/ô/	draw
/h/	hat	/i/	hit	/ēə/	rear
/j/	jump	/ī/	ride	/üə/	sure
/k/	kick	/o/	hop	*Diagrams/Digraphs*	
/l/	laugh	/ō/	rope	/zh/	measure
/m/	milk	/oo/	look	/ch/	chick
/n/	no	/u/	cut	/sh/	shout
/p/	pot	/ū/	cute	/th/	think
/r/	rat	/y//ü/	you	/ng	bring
/s/	sit	/oi/	oil		
/t/	toss	/ow/	how		
/v/	vote	/ə/ (schwa)	syringe		
/w/	walk				
/y/	yak				
/z/	zoo				

It is recommended that some **high-frequency decodable words**, such as *and* and *get*, also be memorized by sight so as to increase reading rate and fluency. There are many lists of such words. The most popular is the Dolch word list, which contains 315 words that are purported to be the most frequently used in English. Early childhood teachers might post some of these high-frequency words around the classroom

for maximum exposure or encourage students to play games with sight word flashcards. Repetition will lead to mastery of these words and will help students read more quickly, fluently, and easily.

Helping students practice phonics can involve a variety of strategies and activities, and these should always be developmentally appropriate for the grade level and differentiated to accommodate students with varying needs and skills. A typical phonics progression may look something like this:

1. mastery of high-frequency letter sounds

2. sounding out CVC words

3. mastery of all letter sounds

4. introduction of consonant blends and digraphs

5. long vowel sounds

6. vowel teams

7. *r*-controlled vowels

8. more advanced word parts (e.g., prefixes, suffixes)

9. silent letters

Phonics study is generally undertaken first at the word level. As students move beyond needing to sound out each phoneme or each word, they generally begin reading sentences. Using **connected texts**, or groups of related sentences, is also part of phonics learning and helps students experience learning to read in more authentic contexts.

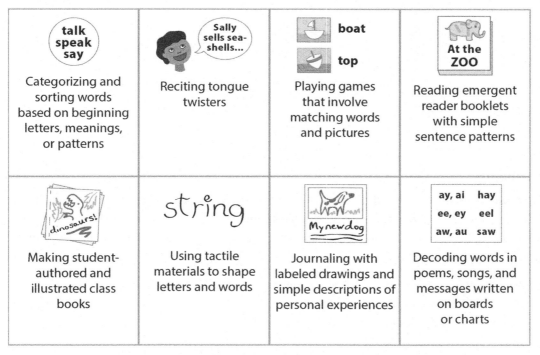

Figure 2.4. Phonics Classroom Strategies

English language learners will need additional practice with phonemes that are unique to English or simply not part of their home languages. Students who come from backgrounds with languages that do not use

the Latin alphabet may need more background with the alphabetic principle than native speakers. Strategies, such as visual cueing to indicate certain sounds, may also be needed to help students who are hard of hearing master phonics.

Teachers may also need to provide extension and application activities for gifted students who may become bored with phonics study if they are already reading at a high level of proficiency. Frequently, these students can be accommodated within an existing lesson framework. For example, a teacher may aim for the bulk of her students to master two sight words per week from the Dolch list, but students who already know the whole list might practice spelling these words instead.

There are many types of phonics-based instruction, each with its pros and cons and each with its advocates and opponents. Some methods may work better with particular students or particular instructional scenarios; however, the main goal of any phonics approach is to aid students in decoding words they encounter while reading.

Practice Questions

4) A teacher says, "hat" and instructs students to produce the sounds they hear in the word. Which strategy is the teacher using to build phoneme awareness?

    A. phoneme blending

    B. phoneme deletion

    C. phoneme segmentation

    D. phoneme substitution

5) Which word is MOST likely a non-decodable word?

    A. atlas

    B. flute

    C. sign

    D. save

Synthetic Phonics

Synthetic phonics is one of the most common and effective types of phonics instruction. At its most basic level, synthetic phonics is associated with students "sounding out" unknown words as part of the decoding or meaning-making process. As students do this, they synthesize the sounds in the words to make meaning, hence the term *synthetic*.

With synthetic phonics, students are explicitly taught to break down words into their component phonemes and sound them out. For example, a student would sound out the word *sheep* based on its three distinct phonemes: /sh/ /ee/ /p/.

Synthetic phonics discourages the practice of guessing at words based on initial letter sound (a common habit among many early readers) or other context or picture cues. It also teaches spelling and reading in tandem, with students sounding out or segmenting words before spelling them.

Synthetic phonics provides an explicit framework for decoding and allows students to tackle most words reliably; however, it is not without disadvantages. Some students rely far too long on the strategy of sounding out, and this can slow down reading rate and fluency and thus overall comprehension.

Practice Question

6) A teacher is working with a student to read the following sentence "He ran to the woods." The student becomes stuck on the word *woods*. Which question should the teacher ask in order to stay aligned with synthetic phonics instruction?

    A. What do the pictures tell you this word might be?

    B. What sound do the letters in the word make?

    C. Where would someone run?

    D. What other words do you know that rhyme with *wood*?

Analytic Phonics

Analytic phonics, or implicit phonics, does not involve sounding out each phoneme in a word; instead, students identify an initial (onset) sound and rime and recognize word families. They do this by applying knowledge from previously learned words or phonograms (symbols representing sounds like /th/ as a representation of the sound they make). Furthermore, whole words are introduced first, and then they are broken into their component parts to determine similarities. (E.g., The words *pin*, *pig*, *play*, and *pride* all have the same initial sound.)

Analytic phonics has its shortcomings. Students are encouraged to guess at words (based on initial letter sound/known structures/context clues), so accuracy may be diminished. This method also relies on students drawing connections by themselves and is less explicit, making it challenging for some learners to pick up analytic phonics as quickly as they do synthetic phonics.

Practice Question

7) Compared with synthetic phonics, analytic phonics relies more on which of the following?

    A. letter-sound correspondence

    B. phoneme blending

    C. knowledge of syllables

    D. context clues

Analogy-Based Phonics

Analogy-based phonics, or **analogy phonics**, teaches students to decode new words based on known words. It is used as part of an analytic phonics approach and is sometimes used in isolation.

Analogy phonics often relies on student familiarity with rimes in words. For example, if a student knows the word *think*, he can use this knowledge to decode similar words like *drink*, *wink*, and *sink*. Like analytic

phonics, analogy-based phonics is often criticized for encouraging guessing and relying on student recall or memorization that may not be applicable in all situations.

Practice Question

8) Which instructional aid is MOST likely to be used in an analogy-based phonics lesson?

    A. a letter-sound chart

    B. a high-frequency word list

    C. a word families chart

    D. a picture dictionary

Embedded Phonics

Embedded phonics, or phonics through context, is an approach to phonics instruction that relies on incidental learning. In this method, whole texts are the primary curricular resources. Explicit phonics instruction is only used when students have trouble reading a particular word. Once that word is decoded, explicit instruction ceases. This approach is often used with the "whole-language" or "whole-word" method of reading instruction, in which reading is considered a natural process that is an outgrowth of presenting children with appropriate texts.

Embedded phonics is also somewhat controversial, as it is neither systematic nor linear. Because specific phonics structures are only taught as needed, more complex structures might appear first. Other structures—often those containing less-used vowel sounds—may never be explicitly taught at all.

Practice Question

9) A preschool has an emergent curriculum that supports reading as a process that students must come to naturally. Why would this preschool MOST likely use embedded phonics instruction?

    A. because it relies on an unpredictable sequence

    B. because it encourages the use of hands-on learning

    C. because it works better for advanced learners

    D. because it can adapt to any text learners choose

Phonics Through Spelling

Phonics through spelling is a combined approach whereby reading and spelling are taught in tandem. Students are taught to spell words phonetically by sounding them out or breaking them into their individual phonemes. The practice is based on the interconnectedness between the sounds of words and their spellings. This interconnectedness is what allows for **invented spelling**, whereby children learn to spell by spelling all words phonetically. For example, they might spell *different* as *difrint*.

The advantage of this approach is that spelling is taught early and alongside reading. Many educators believe invented spelling is a natural part of the learning-to-write process; however, some critics argue

that a total phonetic spelling approach fails to account for all of the nuances of the English language. For example, a student using this approach exclusively might spell *phone* as *fone*.

Practice Question

10) Why will students need to deviate from the exclusive use of a phonics-through-spelling model at some point in their academic careers?

    A. because not all words are spelled phonetically

    B. because it is only applicable to single-syllable words

    C. because the method does not address reading skills

    D. because it requires students to work in collaborative groups

Best Practices for Teaching Phonics

Research indicates that a synthetic phonics approach is the most universal method of phonics instruction that can meet the needs of the most learners. Research also indicates that **systematic phonics instruction** that occurs in a particularly designed sequence is most effective. Typical approaches to explicit, systematic synthetic phonics instruction involve

- teaching individual letter sounds,
- teaching consonant blends,
- teaching consonant digraphs, and
- teaching irregular/challenging vowel sounds (e.g., *r*-controlled vowels).

When learning more advanced phonics structures, like blends and digraphs, students will need explicit instruction since these are multiple letters that make a single sound. This is done through a combination of modeling and then guided and independent practice. At the early childhood levels (typically preschool to grade two or three), educators use small-group instruction to work with students more closely and provide more targeted oral feedback.

Research also shows that phonics instruction is most effective when it also includes **connected texts**, or words in sentences and paragraphs instead of only in isolation or lists.

> **Did You Know?**
>
> Research draws a correlation between a teacher's knowledge of phonics and that teacher's effectiveness in teaching it. Reading specialists are often called on to increase teacher knowledge of phonics, particularly for teachers in early childhood classrooms.

These texts can be chosen for practice and reinforcement with a particular skill or phonics structure and can allow students to practice new skills in an authentic context.

Practicing phonics skills in connected texts is different from using an embedded phonics approach. In embedded phonics, phonics is only taught explicitly when there is a breakdown in the understanding of the connected texts. In a systematic, explicit phonics approach, phonetic structures are first introduced in isolation through direct instruction and practice. Only after this are connected texts introduced. Phonics word patterns are introduced in sequence based on their degrees of difficulty (numbered below in ascending order from least to most difficult):

1.   VC or CVC words with simple (continuous) initial sounds (e.g., *man, pat, fin, at, on*)

2.   VCC or CVCC words with initial continuous sounds (e.g., *ask, mash*)

3.   CVC words with initial stop sounds (e.g., *cab, hit*)

4.   CCVC words (Easier blends with continuous sounds are generally taught before more challenging blends with stop sounds; e.g., *flat, slap, stop, crab*.)

5.   CCVCC, CCCVC, or CCCVCC words with various levels of complexity are then introduced, including consonant digraphs (e.g., /sh/ /ch/) and vowel combinations (e.g., *ee, ea, oo*) as well as *r*-controlled vowels like *butter, wither, firm, germ*, etc.

While it is unlikely to find an entire text that contains only VC or CVC words—or even only decodable words—shared/paired/choral reading strategies can help make texts accessible to all learners. Furthermore, explicit practice with high-frequency sight words alongside phonics instruction is recommended. Instant recognition of common words will make decoding connected texts easier, faster, and more enjoyable for young readers. Above all, explicit and systematic phonics instruction should be calibrated for each student but should always aim at giving students the most useful and widely needed skills first. By doing this, even young children can begin reading independently early on, building confidence and possibly a lifelong love of reading.

Practice Question

11) Which word is the MOST difficult for students to decode and would thus be introduced toward the end of the phonics continuum?

    A.   dirt

    B.   stop

    C.   call

    D.   flat

Assessing Phonics Skills

In addition to more structured assessment methods, like charts and lists, phonics skills can be assessed through any number of hands-on activities. Students can play with letter/sound cards or magnets and form or dissect words. Students can match up cards with different rimes and onsets or different target consonant or vowel sounds.

When assessing decoding—the ability to sound out a word and glean meaning—an oral assessment approach continues to be the gold standard. There are many assessment tools designed specifically to aid in assessing such skills, including the popular **Quick Phonics Screener (QPS)**, which assesses a student's ability to read a variety of sounds and words.

It is important to note student strengths and weaknesses when assessing their decoding skills; however, teachers must also develop a general idea of a student's overall approach and "word-attack skills," or methods of decoding unfamiliar words. Attention to how students approach any oral reading task can provide significant information on strategies they are already using as well as those they do not use but might find beneficial. Though the age of the student certainly comes into play, sometimes older students

still mastering decoding might be able to verbalize the way they approach such challenging words. Questions posed to the student about strategy or method can also yield valuable information.

In addition to these methods, there are also several published assessment instruments for pre-readers and emerging readers:

- Letter knowledge and phonemic awareness can be assessed using the **Dynamic Indicators of Basic Early Literacy Skills (DIBELS)** and the **Early Reading Diagnostic Assessment (ERDA)**.
- The **Comprehensive Test of Phonological Processing (CTOPP)** and **Phonological Awareness Test (PAT)** can also be used as instruments to assess phonemic awareness.
- Other instruments that assess early reading skills include the **Texas Primary Reading Inventory (TPRI)**, **Test of Word Reading Efficiency (TOWRE)**, and even the kindergarten version of the **Iowa Test of Basic Skills (ITBS)**.

Regardless of the assessment instruments used, assessing emerging readers can be challenging since young children often find assessment scenarios intimidating. Any single assessment is only as useful as the portion of the full picture that it provides. The fullest picture of a student's pre-reading development can best be gleaned through observation and input from both parents and teachers. Portfolios, observational records, checklists, and other informal assessment methods can provide much insight into the development of emergent readers.

Practice Question

12) A kindergarten teacher wants to quickly assess a new student's familiarity with sounding out CVC words. In order to accomplish this, which word should the teacher ask the student to sound out?

A. gap

B. onto

C. drink

D. and

Sight Words

Some words deviate from basic sound structures and cannot be sounded out. These words should be presented to students frequently so they can be memorized. Such terms must become **sight words**, or words that require no decoding because they are instantly recognized and read automatically. Some high-frequency decodable words, such as *get*, *and*, and *as* should also be memorized by sight to increase reading rate and fluency.

There are many lists of sight words. The most popular is the **Dolch word list**, which contains 315 words determined to be the most frequently used in English. Early childhood teachers might post some of these high-frequency words around the classroom or encourage students to play games with sight word flashcards. Repetition will lead to mastery of these words and will help students read more quickly, fluently, and easily. Many state and national standards require students to recognize and read from a research-based list. Some states and districts provide such lists to parents and students for practice at home.

Did You Know?

Fifty percent of all written material is made up of only one hundred of the most used words.

The balance between phonics and sight words is important. Students whose only reading strategy is sounding out may continue this even when they come across a word they know. This prevents automaticity and slows reading rate and, subsequently, comprehension. As students become more proficient readers, they should be encouraged to say words they know by sight or memory automatically without having to sound them out.

Educators should provide plenty of opportunities for students to be exposed to and read high-frequency words. Students can practice targeted activities aimed at memorization (such as paired drills or group activities) and read a variety of texts with these words. When students get stuck on high-frequency sight words, teachers can practice the "I say, you say, we say" method for immediate reinforcement.

Practice Question

13) Why are sight words unlike other words that early readers encounter?

    A. because they lack typical structures that allow for sounding out

    B. because they appear infrequently and only in certain genres

    C. because they have multiple meanings based on context

    D. because they should be memorized and recognized instantly

Spelling

Spelling Development

Students typically begin to write and spell simple words as they are developing other language skills, such as speaking, listening, and reading; however, it is important to view spelling as part of a developmental continuum and not overemphasize correct spelling too early when preschool students are still forming mock letters or letter strings. A standard **continuum of spelling** (see Table 2.6.) can be referenced to tailor spelling instruction appropriate to grade level while always keeping in mind the differing developmental levels within a classroom.

Table 2.6. The Continuum of Spelling	
By the end of first grade, most students should be able to correctly spell short words with . . .	• short vowel sounds with a consonant-verb-consonant (*cat*, *dog*, *pin*) pattern [CVC]; • vowel-consonant pattern (*up*, *egg*) and [VC]; • simple consonant-vowel pattern (*go*, *no*) [CV]; and • consonant blends and digraphs in simple and high-frequency words (*chat*, *that*) [CCVC].
By the end of second grade, most students should be spelling words with . . .	• final consonant blends (*rant*, *fast*, *bend*, *link*) [CVCC]; • regular long vowel patterns (*ride*, *tube*) [CVC];

Table 2.6. The Continuum of Spelling

	• double consonant endings (*lick*, *fuss*); • more complex long vowel patterns (*suit*, *fail*); and • r-controlled vowels (*near*, *bear*, *hair*, *are*).
By the end of third grade, most students should be able to spell words with . . .	• non-*r*-controlled but other consonants that influence vowels (*stall*, *draw*); • diphthongs (*coil*, *soon*, *enjoy*, *wow*); • soft *g*'s and *c*'s (*dice*, *hedge*); • short vowel patterns (*head*, *sought*); • silent consonants (*tomb*, *known*, *gnaw*, *wrote*); • advanced digraphs and blends (*phase*, *character*, *whose*); • contractions; • two-syllable words; • compound words; • words with suffixes that show number or degree (*fastest*, *foxes*); and • special spelling rules such as doubling the final letter on CVC words when adding certain suffixes (*napping*, *saddest*).

Explicit spelling instruction will generally begin with simple consonant-vowel-consonant (CVC) patterns and progress as students learn new phonics structures. Practice with **homophones**, or words that have the same pronunciation but different spellings and meanings, should begin in third grade—or sooner—for some students. Common homophones include *there/their/they're*, *to/two/too*, and so on. It is important to point out to students that software applications that might detect spelling errors in other words often fail to pick up on spelling errors with homophones, so students should be extra vigilant when editing and revising writing that contains these words.

> **Did You Know?**
>
> Diphthongs are sounds created by two vowels together, such as in the word *oil*.

Knowledge of spelling rules or patterns is also important. Some of these, such as the following, are **position-based patterns:**

- The letter *i* comes before the letter *e* (except when a long sound is present).

- When there is a vowel blend (e.g., /ee/ea/ai/oa), the sound made is typically a long vowel sound based on the first letter.

1. Foundations of Language

- When there is a vowel-consonant-*e* pattern (e.g., *take* or *rate*), the vowel is usually long.

Other spelling rules are based on suffixes:

- Drop a silent *e* before adding any suffix that begins with a vowel (e.g., *give/giving*).

- Keep the *e* when the suffix starts with a consonant (e.g.,. *use/useful*).

- Drop the *y* when adding a suffix (e.g., *baby/babies*).

Other common spelling rules can be learned and taught with word families, such as words that end in *-ion* (*vacation, station, decision*) or words that end in *-ck*, such as luck, duck, and struck.

Practice Question

14) Which word has a CVC pattern?
    A. gap
    B. onto
    C. drink
    D. and

Spelling Instruction

Spelling instruction should be explicit and systematic, focusing on **orthographic knowledge**, or an understanding of the system by which spoken language is communicated in writing. To develop orthographic knowledge, students must have certain foundational skills based on an understanding of the three layers of linguistic information:

- alphabetic: recognition of letter-sound correspondence and sounding out from left to right
- pattern: understanding more complex patterns that might not be simple left to right, such as long vowel digraphs or open and closed syllables
- meaning: understanding meaning in word parts that do not change with pronunciation, such as *sign* and *signature*

To spell, students need skills in visualization and auditory sequencing. **Visualization** is the ability to recall the spelling of a word and write it based on a stored mental image. **Auditory sequencing** is the ability to identify a word's sounds in the proper order. These skills are linked to both reading and spelling proficiency and are important foundations.

There are three primary approaches to spelling instruction.

- The **basal approach** is rooted in the notion of **orthographic patterns**, or spelling generalizations. These include consonant doubling, adding prefixes and suffixes, dropping the silent *e* when adding a suffix, and so on. This approach involves a set curriculum with spelling lists that gradually increase in difficulty. Research suggests that these lists are most effective when grouped by orthographic pattern and when they contain high-frequency words that students can decode when reading.
- The **developmental approach** involves individualizing spelling instruction based on the developmental level and needs of individual students. This approach uses the research-backed

strategies of the basal approach but does not rely on a single spelling list or spelling continuum or curriculum for all students. The developmental approach is gaining in popularity and is characterized by practices like focusing on words that are within a student's instructional level, defined by a list of words that students can spell with 40 – 90 percent accuracy.

- The **incidental approach**, sometimes called the student-oriented or student-centered approach, teaches spelling in an authentic context. Instead of using a published curriculum, it relies on words students encounter in reading across the content areas. This method is less effective than the other two approaches, but it is still used in some programs that employ a whole-language literacy approach.

Spelling instruction should focus on instruction and assessment. Examples of research-backed spelling instructional activities include the following:

- word sorts: Students sort words based on orthographic features. For example, students might sort words with long and short vowel sounds or words that end in –*ch*.
- phonogram study: Students practice reading and writing words that contain certain sounds, like /ou/, or word endings, like –*ink*.
- writing sorts: Students divide spelling words into columns based on similar orthographic patterns.
- spelling notebooks: Students learn a spelling rule (or exception to it) and then list words that demonstrate it.
- cover-copy-compare: Students study word spellings, cover them up, and then spell them independently, checking afterward for accuracy.

It is important to provide opportunities for students to apply spelling skills in writing. Students can write a paragraph or essay using words from a spelling list or words with a certain orthographic pattern. Students must be explicitly taught that the purpose of studying spelling is to become a competent writer, not a perfect speller. Students must receive many opportunities to *apply* spelling skills as part of the drafting and revision processes.

Regardless of specific activities and approaches, educators should assess spelling proficiency in multiple contexts. This means that assessment of student progress should not rely solely on traditional spelling tests; it should include authentic assessments, both formal and informal, as educators monitor students' overall writing development.

Practice Question

15) A second-grade teacher is planning a unit on plural nouns. Which spelling rule would be MOST appropriate to introduce?

- A. drop the *y* when adding a suffix
- B. double the final consonant when adding -*ing*
- C. keep a silent *e* when a suffix begins with a consonant
- D. consider the phonemes in a word before writing it

Answer Key

1) B: Knowing the difference between a letter, a word, and a sentence is an important component of print awareness, and asking a student to point to a specific sentence is the answer option that would best help gauge a student's print awareness.

2) B: Teaching certain patterns in the English language helps students become strong decoders because they will be able to recognize those patterns when they encounter unfamiliar words.

3) D: The morpheme *un-* is both derivational (can create a new word when added) and bound (must be added to another morpheme).

4) C: The strategy of phoneme segmentation requires students to separate the phonemes in a word.

5) C: The word *sign* deviates from standard phonics structures. The fact that the /g/ is not pronounced and the /i/ is a long vowel sound must simply be memorized.

6) B: Asking about the sounds the letters make will help the student decode the word *woods* by sounding it out.

7) D: Analytic phonics encourages readers to guess at words by using context without sounding out each phoneme.

8) C: In an analogy-based phonics lesson, students use knowledge of word families to aid in decoding. For example, a student who knows *lug, bug,* and *tug* can build on this knowledge to decode *shrug*.

9) D: In an emergent curriculum, students determine the course of the curriculum and would likely choose their own reading materials. This means that whatever utilitarian phonics skills they need to decode a text could be taught as needed with an embedded phonics approach.

10) A: One of the disadvantages of this method is that more complex words cannot be spelled phonetically.

11) A: The word *dirt* contains an *r*-controlled vowel, which is one of the most challenging structures.

12) A: The pattern is *g* (consonant), *a* (vowel), and *p* (consonant).

13) D: Sight words should be memorized for instant recognition in order to aid in automaticity.

14) A: The pattern is *g* (consonant) *a* (vowel) *p* (consonant).

15) A: This would apply to many plural words (e.g., ladies, babies).

3. Word Analysis and Vocabulary Development

Word Analysis

The human brain uses three cueing systems to determine the meaning of words: semantic, syntactic, and graphophonetic. Together, these systems form word-analysis strategies, or **word-attack strategies**, which are methods of decoding unfamiliar words.

Semantic (Meaning) Cues

Semantic cues are cues to a word's meaning drawn from background knowledge or prior experience. Semantic cues are the brain's most efficient cueing system since words are immediately retrieved from memory and processed. Semantic cues rely on students to activate knowledge and make reasonable predictions and inferences regarding a word's meaning. For example, in an informational text on fishing, the word *bobber* might come up. A reader familiar with fishing could activate this knowledge and recognize that the term *bobber* refers to a float used on a fishing line.

Semantic cueing is used in **cloze exercises** in which words are removed from the text and students must supply them. Some strategies to activate students' background knowledge to allow for maximum semantic cueing include the following:

- using metacognitive strategies and questions like "What type of word would make sense here?"; "Does this meaning make sense in a text about _____?"; "What qualities do _____ have that might lead to a clue of this word's meaning?"

- having students make a list of words they predict might be used in the text after previewing its title, illustrations, and headings

- engaging students in scripted exercises in which they confirm predictions, such as "The word _____ must mean _____ because I know that _____."

Semantic cues can also be based on the text itself. These are called context clues and do not necessarily have to be integrated with existing background knowledge. **Context clues** are any cues that help readers determine word meaning in connected texts, and they can be other words in the text or graphics. Students should be explicitly taught to identify other words in a sentence, paragraph, or passage that provide possible clues to the meaning of an unknown word. Students of all ages can also look to illustrations or charts to understand new words. This is particularly helpful with subject-specific vocabulary, such as terminology associated with organelles within plant cells.

Other words in the text are also essential in decoding **homographs** (words that are spelled the same but have different meanings) and **homonyms** (words that sound the same and may or may not be spelled the same but have different meanings). Educators often teach decoding homonyms and homographs explicitly. Teachers should direct students to the most commonly used homonyms in order to prepare them for encountering such words in texts.

Context is usually the only way to determine the meaning of a homograph or multiple-meaning word. Homonyms can, at times, be decoded based on spelling alone, presuming the spelling differs, but this method should always be confirmed based on context to ensure correct decoding and understanding. Students can be asked to circle, underline, or highlight the other words in the text that "back up" their interpretations of multiple-meaning words.

Practice Question

1) Which activity would MOST likely help students develop the knowledge to use semantic cues effectively?

    A. reading books that provide information on a variety of places and cultures

    B. underlining confusing sentences and diagramming them

    C. reading a text aloud twice: once to oneself and once to a partner

    D. encouraging students to increase their reading rate to retain more information

Syntactic (Structural) Cues

Syntactic cues are based on the structure of language and are regarded as the brain's second-most efficient cueing system while reading. They include sentence structure and word order, structural clues within words, and structural analysis of the word.

A word's meaning can sometimes be clued or determined by its placement in a sentence. For example, figuring out whether a word is used as an adjective, noun, or verb can help with determining its meaning.

Structural clues within words, such as affixes (prefixes and suffixes) and roots (base words with no affixes), can give clues to a word's meaning. Using structural clues is sometimes referred to as **morphemic analysis**, or the analysis of morphemes (the smallest units of meaning within words). Tables 3.1. and 3.2. contain some of the most common roots and affixes.

Students should be taught common Greek and Latin roots and their meanings as well as the meanings of common prefixes and suffixes. Students can practice roots and affixes by creating words with a single prefix like *geo* (e.g., *geography, geology, geopolitical, geoscience*) or with a single suffix like *–ly* (e.g., *friendly, happily, angrily*). Students can then determine what all the words they have created have in common. Students can also be given roots and asked to create as many new words with affixes as possible. Students should then be encouraged to transfer this knowledge when they encounter new words in texts by using known roots or affixes as clues to the word's meaning.

Structural analysis of the word can also be a useful strategy. Students can decode compound words, for example, by breaking the word into its two component parts.

Table 3.1. Common Roots and Affixes

Root	Definition	Example
ast(er)	star	asteroid, astronomy
audi	hear	audience, audible
auto	self	automatic, autograph
bene	good	beneficent, benign
bio	life	biology, biorhythm
cap	take	capture
ced	yield	secede
chrono	time	chronicle, chronic
corp	body	corporeal
crac *or* crat	rule	autocrat
demo	people	democracy
dict	say	dictionary, dictation
duc	lead or make	abduct, produce
gen	give birth	generation, genetics
geo	earth	geography, geometry
grad	step	graduate
graph	write	graphical, autograph
ject	throw	eject
jur or jus	law	justice, jurisdiction
log or logue	thought	logic, logarithm
luc	light	lucid

Table 3.1. Common Roots and Affixes

Root	Definition	Example
man	hand	manual
mand	order	demand
mis	send	transmission
mono	one	monotone
omni	all	omnivore
path	feel	pathology
phil	love	philanthropy
phon	sound	phonograph
port	carry	export
qui	rest	quiet
scrib or script	write	scribe, transcript
sense or sent	feel	sentiment
tele	far away	telephone
terr	earth	terrace
uni	single	unicode
vac	empty	vacant
vid	see	video
vis	see	vision

Table 3.2. Common Prefixes

Prefix	Definition	Example
a- (also an-)	not, without; to, toward; of, completely	atheist, anemic, aside, aback, anew, abashed
ante-	before, preceding	antecedent, anteroom
anti-	opposing, against	antibiotic, anticlimax
com- (also co-, col-, con-, cor-)	with, jointly, completely	combat, codriver, collude, confide
dis- (also di-)	negation, removal	disadvantage, disbar
en- (also em-)	put into or on; bring into the condition of; intensify	engulf, entomb
hypo-	under	hypoglycemic, hypothermia
in- (also il-, im-, ir-)	not, without; in, into, toward, inside	infertile, impossible, influence, include
intra-	inside, within	intravenous, intrapersonal
out-	surpassing, exceeding; external, away from	outperform, outdoor
over-	excessively, completely; upper, outer, over, above	overconfident, overcast
pre-	before	precondition, preadolescent, prelude
re-	again	reapply, remake
semi-	half, partly	semicircle, semiconscious
syn- (also sym-)	in union, acting together	synthesis, symbiotic
trans-	across, beyond	transatlantic
trans-	into a different state	translate
under-	beneath, below	underarm, undersecretary

Table 3.2. Common Prefixes		
Prefix	**Definition**	**Example**
under-	not enough	underdeveloped

Practice Question

2) A student is stuck on the word *Istanbul* in the following sentence "My father took a trip to Istanbul." She asks, "What is an Istanbul?" How can the teacher BEST encourage the student to use syntactic cues to help determine the word's meaning?

    A. have her break the word into its three syllables and sound out each syllable individually

    B. ask her if she has ever been to Turkey and, if so, what cities she visited

    C. cover up *Istanbul* and ask her what kind of word would most likely go in the blank

    D. ask her if she thinks the sentence makes sense as written or if the word *Istanbul* should be moved

Graphophonic Cues

The **graphophonic cueing** system is based on applying sound (phoneme)-symbol (grapheme or letter) knowledge while reading. It is the most basic level of decoding and tends to be the least efficient since its focus is on individual units (e.g., letters and letter patterns) instead of larger chunks of text like words and ideas.

One common word-attack strategy based on graphophonics is knowledge of syllabication and syllable patterns. Students can be taught to break words into syllables and then identify the six syllable patterns to aid in decoding:

    1. **Closed syllables** are the most common. They end in a consonant that causes the vowel to make a short sound. *Stretch*, *com*-puter, *bat*, and *backing* are all words with closed syllables and short vowel sounds.

    2. **Open syllables** end in vowels and make long vowel sounds. *Ri*-val, *mi-cro*-phone, and *to*-tal are all examples of open syllables.

    3. **Vowel-consonant-e syllables**, or VCE syllables, end in –e, which makes the final vowel sound long. De-*code*, *rude*, *bake* all have VCE syllables.

    4. **Vowel teams** are two vowels next to each other that make a single sound. Some vowel teams are digraphs (only two letters), and others consist of three or four letters. L*augh*, h*igh*, and h*ay* are examples of vowel teams.

    5. **Consonant–le syllables**, or C–*le* syllables, are also sometimes called **final syllables** or **final stable syllables**. When these endings are joined with an open syllable, there is a long vowel sound

and no double consonant. When they are joined with a closed syllable, there is a short vowel sound and double consonant. There are eleven –le patterns in English: –ble (trouble), –gle (struggle), –zle (dazzle), –fle (trifle), –tle (battle), –dle (idle), –stle (whistle), –ckle (buckle), –ple (triple), –cle (recycle), and –kle (wrinkle).

6. **R-controlled syllables**, also called vowel-r syllables, are often the most challenging. With these types of constructions, a vowel is followed by the letter r, which changes the way the vowel is pronounced. For example, in the word water, the final syllable is not pronounced as a purely short e because it is an r-controlled vowel. Research suggests that explicit instruction and practice with r-controlled vowel forms (er, ir, ur, ar, or) and frequent repetition and review is essential to help students master these types of sounds to aid in decoding.

For graphophonic cueing to be most effective, readers must have some knowledge of the word they sound out in order to make meaning. For example, a first-grade student might be able to apply graphophonic cueing to successfully sound out the word telepathy and might figure out the correct pronunciation of this word while reading orally or even silently; however, this word is not truly decoded, or has meaning taken from it, unless the student can apply the graphophonic cues to existing knowledge of oral language vocabulary.

For this reason, many educators employ the **language experience approach (LEA)**. In this approach to literacy instruction, word recognition is thought to come not from graphophonic cues but rather from words that have been experienced and written about by the students and teacher. This and other similar approaches are called **whole-language** instruction, which does not use any cueing system smaller than the word level. This is the antithesis of phonics and graphophonic cueing: in a whole-language approach, students must use semantic and syntactic cues as the only methods for decoding new words.

Practice Question

3) Which word contains BOTH an open syllable and an r-controlled vowel?
   A. rigorous
   B. related
   C. hunger
   D. miser

Vocabulary Development

While fluency is essential for reading to learn, students also need vocabulary knowledge to comprehend what they read. Children learn vocabulary in a variety of ways, including repeated exposure in speech and print and through explicit instruction.

In a literacy-rich classroom, students will be exposed to a wide variety of vocabulary, and teachers can further aid vocabulary acquisition by incorporating new words and new meanings into the daily classroom routine. Some vocabulary acquisition will involve learning **content-specific words** that require students to first understand the vocabulary of the subject before applying the knowledge. Consider that even a kindergarten student must master dozens of basic math terms before applying them. For example, the terms triangle, hexagon, and rectangle must all be learned intrinsically before a student can separate or

sort items by shape. Additionally, third graders must learn terms like *habitat, natural resource, metric system,* and *variable* to be able to apply them to science and math assignments.

Student vocabulary must also grow to include the various homonyms, or **multiple-meaning words**, that exist in the English language. The word *interest*, for example, might mean one thing as it applies to a math unit on saving money and another when used in a freewriting assignment on a topic of *interest*.

As students progress in vocabulary development, they will also begin to consider the difference between the **denotative**, or literal meaning of a word, and its **connotative**, or more subtle meaning. For example, the word *take* literally means to reach for and obtain something, but the word's connotation is different from the word *snatch*, which, though it has a similar denotative meaning, implies a more negative action. Connotative meanings may be challenging for English language learners to glean at first, so such students may need scaffolding and supports built into lessons that are aimed at word connotations.

Practice Question

4) Which word has a potential negative connotation?

   A. skim

   B. read

   C. immerse

   D. study

Vocabulary can—and should—be broadened through a variety of strategies. Vocabulary knowledge makes reading more expedient and fluent since readers can simply decode a word semantically without having to resort to other cueing systems. Vocabulary is developed through one of two ways:

- **Incidental vocabulary learning** occurs while reading, either independently or through teacher-guided oral reading activities.
- **Intentional vocabulary learning** requires educators to more explicitly direct vocabulary acquisition. There are two methodologies to intentional vocabulary teaching:
    - specific word instruction
    - word-learning strategies

Specific Word Instruction

Specific word instruction involves activities that help learners acquire knowledge of new words. The following are just some strategies for specific word instruction:

- **Predict-O-Gram:** Students are given a list of words and then predict how those words will be used in a text. This strategy can be used effectively for both fiction and nonfiction texts, though it is most often used with fiction since it can easily be integrated into existing knowledge about plot structure.

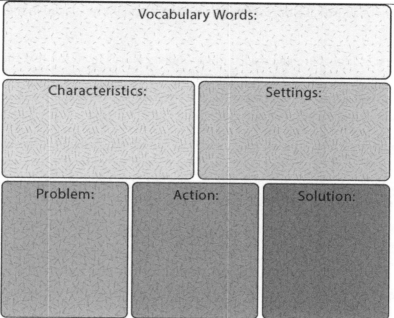

Figure 3.1. Predict-O-Gram

- **Semantic impressions:** Students are given a list of words in the order in which they appear in the text. The definition of each word is then briefly discussed by the teacher. Students write their own story using the words in the same order, using each word only once. They then read the text and compare their finished story to the original.

- **Semantic feature analysis**, also called a semantic grid, is a graphic organizer that helps students think deeply about the features or properties of each vocabulary word.

Semantic Feature Analysis Grid

Category: _____

Terms | Features/Properties

Figure 3.2. Semantic Feature Analysis

list-group-label is a semantic mapping strategy in which students brainstorm all the words they can think of that relate to a particular topic. They then divide the list of words into subcategories based on common

features. For example, words like *dorsal fin*, *gills*, and *teeth* might be placed in the category of "parts of a fish's body."

possible sentences: Students are given a list of vocabulary words from the text they will read. They then write a "possible" sentence for each word, illustrating the word's possible meaning. After reading the text, students return to their possible sentences to see if they were accurate or if the sentences need to be changed based on the word's actual meaning as revealed in the text.

OPIN (short for *opinion*) is similar to a cloze exercise in which students fill in the blank with a word they think belongs in a sentence. Students then break into groups to "defend" their word choices to other members of the group. This strategy helps reinforce other skills since students use context clues and background knowledge to justify their answers.

Practice Question

5) A professional development event is being organized to discuss ways to incorporate creative writing into daily reading instruction. Which vocabulary-building activity is MOST likely to be discussed during this event?

    A. list-group-label

    B. OPIN

    C. semantic impressions

    D. semantic grids

Word-Learning Strategies

In addition to specific word instruction, educators must use various strategies and tools to help students learn new words they encounter. Some of these are discussed below:

In today's digital age, there are many opportunities for students to practice using resources to find the meaning of unfamiliar words. **Dictionary** skills are typically introduced around third grade and require explicit instruction on how to locate the word's pronunciation, etymology, parts of speech, and definition. Students should be taught to use both print and digital dictionaries. Many state standards require this knowledge, which is tested on annual accountability tests.

There are, of course, some limitations to dictionaries. They tend to focus only on a word's **denotation**, or literal meaning, when each word also has a **connotation**, or subtle or implied meaning. Readers must be taught to use context clues to determine connotation.

Thesauruses should also be used in reading and English classrooms. Students should learn when a thesaurus is the resource of choice and when a dictionary is more appropriate. Use of the **glossary** should also be explicitly taught, and students should be encouraged to apply this skill across the content areas since many of their texts for other courses will likely contain glossaries.

Morphemic analysis breaks apart the morphemes within words and analyzes them for meaning. Morphemic analysis should be taught explicitly as a unit of study and referred to frequently throughout reading instruction. Students should be asked to think about unfamiliar words in the context of their

morphemes to help with decoding: "Are there roots or affixes I already know from other words?" "What does the word ending tell me?" "Is it a clue to the part of speech or singularity or plurality?"

Contextual analysis applies context clues to infer the meaning of unknown words. As mentioned above, contextual analysis can involve semantic or syntactic cues that aid in meaning. Some educators find strategies in annotating the text very helpful in teaching context clues. For example, students can put a question mark next to unknown words and then circle other words in the text that might provide clues to the unknown word's meaning.

English language learners will need additional vocabulary-building practice, as vocabulary knowledge is one of the key foundations that leads to reading success for students with little background in English vocabulary. Specific strategies include picture dictionaries, teaching cognates, and teaching idioms, in addition to explicit and direct vocabulary instruction.

Practice Question

6) Which vocabulary term would MOST likely be included in a lesson on dictionary skills in a fourth-grade classroom?

A. noun

B. phonogram

C. context

D. origin

Fluency

Fluency refers to the rate, accuracy, and expression of written text when it is read. Fluency is an important measure of a student's reading development; lack of fluency will hamper overall comprehension as well as the enjoyment of reading. Reading **rate** is a measure of speed and is generally calculated in words per minute. **Accuracy**, or the correct decoding of words, is generally entwined with rate when measuring fluency since reading quickly but incorrectly is not desirable.

In addition to rate and accuracy, **prosody**—the overall liveliness and expressiveness of reading—is also a skill to nurture in students. Prosody may involve appropriate pauses and various changes in pitch and intonation based on punctuation and the overall meaning of the piece. Developing prosody in students should involve a combination of modeling by teachers (e.g., reading stories, passages, and even directions aloud) and giving students plenty of opportunities for oral reading practice.

Many situations can threaten students' fluency: Limited phonics knowledge may cause students to struggle with new or challenging words. Other students may have limited sight word knowledge, which can slow down their reading rates as they sound out each word. Some students may lack vocabulary knowledge or knowledge of academic language. English language learners (ELLs) who are in classrooms with native English speakers may struggle to keep pace with the reading and accuracy rates of their native English-speaking peers.

The overarching instructional strategy for helping students develop fluency is practice, which may involve any of the following strategies:

- modeling oral fluency

  o Peer-assisted learning strategies (PALS), which could involve pairing ELLs with native English speakers, can aid in meeting the needs of ELLs in the context of reading instruction.

- using choral reading exercises where a more proficient reader or teacher reads with the student

- teaching finger tracking while reading or using a tracking device

- rereading the same texts multiple times

- increasing sight word recognition

- increasing phonics knowledge

While fluency is not limited to oral reading, it is virtually impossible to assess fluency during silent reading, and most educators rely on frequent oral reading assessments to help determine student progress. While several standard measures exist, one of the most researched is the Hasbrouck-Tindal oral reading fluency chart. This chart is designed to measure progress over the course of the school year and from grade to grade, and it compares students in percentiles with their peers on a scale of words read correctly per minute. It is important to remember that all students will develop fluency on a different timeline, and assessments of fluency are most accurate when they are developmentally appropriate and when they are not presented as high-stakes testing situations.

Educators may find it challenging to find time for oral reading assessment in the classroom as they balance multiple priorities; however, teachers must make themselves available to regularly listen to all students read aloud, regardless of grade level. While examining written work and performance on independent or group practice activities may give some indication of a student's overall development, teachers must gather as much data as possible in order to get the fullest picture. Assessing student fluency through oral reading is seminal to an overall understanding of a particular student's learning situation.

Fluency is highly correlated with comprehension because students who struggle to read and decode individual words will have difficulty comprehending entire sentences and paragraphs. Additionally, students who read at a very slow rate may have trouble recalling what they have read. It is well worth the time investment to listen to students read aloud as much as possible.

> **Helpful Hint:**
>
> There are various software applications that allow teachers to record and track students' oral reading progress. While this technology cannot replace frequent live listening to students reading, it can augment it and speaks to the importance of oral reading in gauging students' overall literacy development.

Practice Question

7) A second-grade teacher notices that her students often read in monotone during oral reading practice. Which strategy would BEST help the students develop prosody?

A. setting aside timed oral reading each day

B. modeling an appropriate reading rate

C. using ability grouping for silent reading

D. having students act out a play from a script

Answer Key

1) A: Reading a broad array of books builds background knowledge, which can then be applied and retrieved.

2) C: Prompting the student to cover up the word and asking her which type of word would most likely go in the blank will help the student use the sentence's structure to determine that the word *Istanbul* must be a place.

3) D: The term *miser* contains both an open syllable (*mi*) and an *r*-controlled vowel (*ser*).

4) A: Depending on the context in which it is used, the word *skim* could subtly imply that a reader did not read a text in its entirety or that the reader lacked interest in the written piece.

5) C: In semantic impressions, students write a story with the words from the text.

6) D: Most dictionaries include an entry for the word *origin* that students should be taught to use.

7) D: Having students read from a script would give them practice reading expressively.

4. Language and Its Parts

Academic Language

Understanding the structure of language is an important part of effective oral and written communication. Language has many functions:

- emotional expression
- play
- identity expression
- imaginative expression
- communication

Academic language is generally used for communication in a school setting. Depending on their backgrounds, students may have little past experience with academic language.

Students may not consistently use the parts of speech correctly in their writing and speaking until well into their elementary years. Within oral language development, there are phases during which children leave out needed articles, prepositions, and other linking words. Once speech becomes fully developed and students are generating their own sentences and paragraphs, basic rules of grammar can be introduced.

Throughout elementary school, students are introduced to the conventions of Standard English grammar, usage, mechanics, and spelling as tools to facilitate communication and comprehension when writing, speaking, reading, and listening. They learn how to utilize the English language in both formal and informal contexts through exposure to conversational, academic, and content area language. In addition, they build vocabulary by learning how to use context and word structure to determine the meanings of unknown words and phrases. Elementary language arts teachers are responsible for implementing a curriculum and providing feedback that best helps students develop and strengthen these language skills.

> **Check Your Understanding:**
>
> What are the major phases of oral language development?

Practice Question

1) At what stage of speech development can students begin learning about basic grammar?

A. at any stage

B. once they begin leaving out prepositions and necessary linking words

C. once their speech has been fully developed

D. once they can correctly write their name

Parts of Speech

The **parts of speech** are the building blocks of sentences, paragraphs, and entire texts. Grammarians have typically defined eight parts of speech:

- nouns
- pronouns
- verbs
- adverbs
- adjectives
- conjunctions
- prepositions
- interjections

All of these parts of speech play unique roles in the context of a sentence. A fundamental understanding of the parts of speech is therefore necessary for comprehending basic sentence construction.

Though some words fall easily into one category or another, many words can function as different parts of speech based on their usage within a sentence.

Nouns are the words that describe people, places, things, and ideas. Most often, nouns fill the position of subject or object within a sentence. Nouns have several subcategories:

- common nouns (*chair, car, house*)
- proper nouns (*Julie, David*)
- abstract nouns (*love, intelligence, sadness*)
- concrete nouns (*paper clip, bread, person*)
- compound nouns (*brother-in-law, rollercoaster*)
- noncountable nouns (*money, water*)
- countable nouns (*dollars, cubes*)
- verbal nouns (*writing, diving*)

There is much crossover among these subcategories (e.g., *chair* is common, concrete, and countable), and other subcategories do exist.

Pronouns replace nouns in a sentence or paragraph and allow writers to achieve a smooth flow throughout a text by avoiding unnecessary repetition. The unique aspect of the pronoun as a part of speech is that the list of pronouns is finite: while there are innumerable nouns in the English language, the list of pronouns is rather limited in contrast. There are seven types of pronouns:

- **Personal pronouns** act as subjects or objects in a sentence. (*She received a letter; I gave the letter to her.*)
- **Possessive pronouns** indicate possession. (*The apartment is hers, but the furniture is mine.*)
- **Reflexive** or **intensive pronouns** intensify a noun or reflect back upon a noun. (*I myself made the dessert. I made the dessert myself.*)
- **Relative pronouns** begin dependent clauses. Like other pronouns, they may appear in subject or object case, depending on the clause. (*Charlie, who made the clocks, works in the basement.*)
- **Interrogative pronouns** begin questions. (*Who worked last evening?*) These types of pronouns request information about people, places, things, ideas, location, time, means, and purposes.

- **Demonstrative pronouns** point out or draw attention to something or someone. They can also indicate proximity or distance. (*That* *child in the schoolyard is my student. I live in the red house over* *there.*)
- **Indefinite pronouns** simply replace nouns to avoid unnecessary repetition. (*Several* *came to the party to see* *both.*)

Table 4.1. Personal, Possessive, and Reflexive/Intensive Pronouns

Case	First-Person		Second-Person		Third-Person	
	Singular	Plural	Singular	Plural	Singular	Plural
Subject	I	we	you	you (all)	he, she, it	they
Object	me	us	you	you (all)	him, her, it	them
Possessive	mine	ours	yours	yours	his, hers, its	theirs
Reflexive/ Intensive	myself	ourselves	yourself	yourselves	himself, herself, itself	themselves

Table 4.2. Types of Pronouns

Pronoun Type	Pronouns	Example
Relative pronouns	who, whom, which, that, whose	The movie, <u>which</u> opened last weekend, has been very successful.
Interrogative pronouns	who, whom, what, where, when, which, why, how, whose	<u>Which</u> movie would you like to see?
Demonstrative pronouns	this, that, these, those	I saw <u>that</u> movie yesterday.
Indefinite pronouns	each, one, no one, everyone/thing/body, anyone/thing/body, someone/thing/body, both, few, none, all	<u>Everybody</u> went to see the movie last night.

Verbs express action (*run, jump, play*) or state of being (*is, seems*). Verbs that describe action are **action verbs**, and those that describe being are **linking verbs**:

- **action:** My brother <u>plays</u> tennis.
- **linking:** He <u>is</u> the best player on the team.

Verbs are conjugated to indicate **person**, which refers to the point of view of the sentence:

- **First person** is the speaker (*I, we*).
- **Second person** is the person being addressed (*you*).
- **Third person** is outside the conversation (*they, them*).

Verbs are also conjugated to match the **number** (singular or plural) of their subject(s). **Helping verbs** (*to be, to have, to do*) are used to conjugate verbs. An unconjugated verb is called an **infinitive** and includes the word *to* in front (*to be, to break*).

Table 4.3. Verb Conjugation (Present Tense)		
Person Type	**Singular**	**Plural**
First person	I give.	We give.
Second person	You give.	You (all) give.
Third person	He/she/it/ gives.	They give.

Verbs are also conjugated to indicate **tense**, or when an action has happened. Actions can happen in the past, present, or future. Tense also describe the duration of an action:

- **Simple** verbs describe general truths or something that happened once.
- **Continuous** verbs describe ongoing actions.
- **Perfect** verbs describe repeated actions or actions that started in the past and have been completed.
- **Perfect continuous** verbs describe actions that started in the past and are continuing.

Verb Type	Past	Present	Future
Simple	I <u>gave</u> her a gift yesterday.	I <u>give</u> her a gift every day.	I <u>will give</u> her a gift on her birthday.
Continuous	I <u>was giving</u> her a gift when you got here.	I <u>am giving</u> her a gift; come in!	I <u>will be giving</u> her a gift at dinner.
Perfect	I <u>had given</u> her a gift before you got there.	I <u>have given</u> her a gift already.	I <u>will have given</u> her a gift by midnight.
Perfect continuous	Her friends <u>had been giving</u> her gifts all night when I arrived.	I <u>have been giving</u> her gifts every year for nine years.	Next year, I <u>will have been giving</u> her gifts on holidays for ten years.

Table 4.4. Verb Tenses

Check for Understanding:

Identify the type of nouns, pronouns, and verbs used in the following sentence: *Marcus and Paula offered to pick up the cake—they are driving that way anyway—but I told them I would do it myself.*

Verbs that follow the standard rules of conjugation are called **regular** verbs. **Irregular** verbs do not follow these rules, and their conjugations must be memorized. Some examples of irregular verbs are given in Table 4.5.

Table 4.5. Irregular Verbs

Present	Past	Has/Have/Had
am	was	been
do	did	done
see	saw	seen
write	wrote	written
break	broke	broken
grow	grew	grown
speak	spoke	spoken
begin	began	begun
run	ran	run
buy	bought	bought

Transitive verbs take a **direct object**, which receives the action of the verb. **Intransitive verbs** have no object. The person or thing that receives the direct object is the **indirect object**:

- **transitive:** Alex <u>gave</u> the ball to his brother. (*The ball* is the direct object; *his brother* is the indirect object.)
- **intransitive:** She <u>jumped</u> over the fence.

Adjectives modify or describe nouns and pronouns. In English, adjectives are usually placed before the word being modified, although they can also appear after a linking verb, such as *is* or *smells*:

- The <u>beautiful</u> <u>blue</u> <u>jade</u> necklace will go perfectly with my dress.
- I think that lasagna smells <u>delicious</u>.

When multiple adjectives are used, they should be listed in the following order:

1.   determiners: articles (*a*, *an*, and *the*), possessive adjectives (e.g., *my*, *her*), and descriptors of quantity (e.g., *three*, *several*)

2.   opinions: modifiers that imply a value (e.g., *beautiful*, *perfect*, *ugly*)

3.   size: descriptions of size (e.g., *small*, *massive*)

4.   age: descriptions of age (e.g., *young*, *five-year-old*)

5.   shape: descriptions of appearance or character (e.g., *smooth, loud*)

6.   color: descriptions of color (e.g., *blue, dark*)

7.   origin: modifiers that describe where something came from (e.g., *American, homemade*)

8.   material: modifiers that describe what something is made from (e.g., *cotton, metallic*)

9.   purpose: adjectives that function as part of the noun to describe its purpose (e.g., *sewing machine, rocking chair*)

Adverbs, which are often formed by adding the suffix *–ly*, modify any word or set of words that is not a noun or pronoun. They can modify verbs, adjectives, other adverbs, phrases, or clauses:

- He <u>quickly</u> ran to the house next door. (*Quickly* modifies the verb *ran*.)
- Her <u>very</u> effective speech earned her a promotion. (*Very* modifies the adjective *effective*.)
- <u>Finally</u>, the table was set and dinner was ready. (*Finally* modifies the clause *the table was set and dinner was ready*.)

Conjunctions join words into phrases, clauses, and sentences. **Coordinating conjunctions** join two independent clauses and can best be remembered using the acronym *FANBOYS*: <u>f</u>or, <u>a</u>nd, <u>n</u>or, <u>b</u>ut, <u>o</u>r, <u>y</u>et, <u>s</u>o:

- Marta went to the pool, <u>and</u> Alex decided to go shopping.
- Annie didn't want to eat tacos for dinner, <u>so</u> she picked up a pizza on her way home.

> **Check Your Understanding:**
>
> Explain to students that adverbs often answer the question of *how* or *when*. For example, *"She danced." "How* did she dance?" *"She danced <u>beautifully</u>."*

Subordinating conjunctions join dependent clauses to the independent clauses to which they are related:

- We chose that restaurant <u>because</u> Juan loves pizza.

Table 4.6. Subordinating Conjunctions	
Time	after, as, as long as, as soon as, before, since, until, when, whenever, while
Manner	as, as if, as though
Cause	because
Condition	although, as long as, even if, even though, if, provided that, though, unless, while
Purpose	in order that, so that, that
Comparison	as, than

Prepositions set up relationships in time (*after the party*) or space (*under the cushions*) within a sentence. A preposition will always function as part of a prepositional phrase—the preposition along with the object of the preposition.

Interjections have no grammatical attachment to the sentence itself other than to add expressions of emotion. These parts of speech may be punctuated with commas or exclamation points and may fall anywhere within the sentence:

- <u>Ouch</u>! He stepped on my toe.

Practice Questions

2) Identify the underlined part of speech in the following sentence:

Anne and Peter drank their coffee languidly <u>while</u> they read the paper.

    A. subordinating conjunction

    B. irregular verb

    C. coordinating conjunction

    D. adverb

3) Identify the direct object in the following sentence:

My friends brought me a package of souvenirs from their trip to Spain.

    A. friends

    B. me

    C. package

    D. trip

Phrases

A **phrase** is a group of words that communicates a partial idea and lacks either a subject or a predicate. Several phrases may be strung together, one after another, to add detail and interest to a sentence.

Phrases are categorized based on the main word in the phrase. A **prepositional phrase** begins with a preposition and ends with an object of the preposition; a **verb phrase** is composed of the main verb along with its helping verbs; and a **noun phrase** consists of a noun and its modifiers.

- **prepositional phrase:** The dog is hiding <u>under the porch</u>.
- **verb phrase:** The chef <u>would have cooked</u> a different dish, but the diners demanded lasagna.
- **noun phrase:** <u>The big, red barn</u> rests beside <u>the vacant chicken house</u>.

An **appositive phrase** is a particular type of noun phrase that renames the word or group of words that precedes it. Appositive phrases usually follow the noun they describe and are set apart by commas:

- My dad, <u>a clockmaker</u>, loved antiques.

Verbal phrases begin with a word that would normally act as a verb but is instead filling another role within the sentence. These phrases can act as nouns, adjectives, or adverbs:

- **verbal phrase (noun):** <u>To visit Europe</u> had always been her dream.
- **verbal phrase (adjective):** <u>Enjoying the stars that filled the sky</u>, Dave lingered outside for quite a while.

Practice Question

4) Identify the type of phrase underlined in the following sentence:

David, <u>smelling the fresh bread baking</u>, smiled as he woke up.

   A. prepositional phrase

   B. noun phrase

   C. verb phrase

   D. verbal phrase

Clauses and Sentence Structure

Clauses contain both a subject and a predicate. They can be either independent or dependent:

- An **independent** (or main) **clause** can stand alone as its own sentence.
  - Example: The dog ate her homework.
- Dependent (or subordinate) clauses cannot stand alone as their own sentences.
  - They start with a subordinating conjunction, relative pronoun, or relative adjective, which will make them sound incomplete.
  - Example: <u>because</u> the dog ate her homework

Table 4.7. Words That Begin Dependent Clauses	
Subordinating Conjunctions	**Relative Pronouns and Adjectives**
after, before, once, since, until, when, whenever, while, as, because, in order that, so, so that, that, if, even if, provided that, unless, although, even though, though, whereas, where, wherever, than, whether	who, whoever, whom, whomever, whose, which, that, when, where, why, how

Sentences can be classified based on the number and type of clauses they contain. A **simple sentence** will have only one independent clause and no dependent clauses. The sentence may contain phrases, complements, and modifiers, but it will comprise only one independent clause—one complete idea:

- The cat ran under the porch.

A **compound sentence** has two or more independent clauses and no dependent clauses:

- The cat ran under the porch, and the dog ran after him.

A **complex sentence** has only one independent clause and one or more dependent clauses:

- The cat, who is scared of the dog, ran under the porch.

A **compound-complex sentence** has two or more independent clauses and one or more dependent clauses:

- The cat, who is scared of the dog, ran under the porch, and the dog ran after him.

Table 4.8. Sentence Structure and Clauses		
Sentence Structure	**Independent Clauses**	**Dependent Clauses**
Simple	1	0
Compound	2 +	0
Complex	1	1 +
Compound-complex	2 +	1 +

Practice Question

5) Which of the following would be considered a compound sentence?

- A. The turtle swam slowly around the pond.
- B. Alligators generally lie still, but they can move with lightning speed.
- C. Mice are most likely to come at night after other animals have gone to sleep.
- D. Squirrels, to prepare for winter, gather and hide seeds and nuts underground.

Punctuation

Terminal punctuation marks are used to end sentences. The **period** (.) ends declarative (statement) and imperative (command) sentences. The **question mark** (?) terminates interrogative sentences (questions).

Exclamation points end exclamatory sentences, in which the writer or speaker is exhibiting intense emotion or energy:

- **period:** Sarah and I are attending a concert.
- **question mark:** How many people are attending the concert?
- **exclamation point:** That was a great show!

The colon and the semicolon, though often confused, each have a unique set of rules for usage. While both punctuation marks are used to join clauses, the construction of the clauses and the relationship between them is different.

The **semicolon** (;) is used to join two independent clauses (IC; IC) that are closely related:

- I need to buy a new car soon; my old car broke down last month.

The **colon** (:) is used to introduce a list, definition, or clarification. The clause preceding the colon has to be independent, but what follows the colon can be an independent clause, a dependent clause, or a phrase:

- The buffet offers three choices: ham, turkey, or roast beef.
- He decided to drive instead of taking the train: he didn't think the train would arrive in time.

Commas show pauses in the text or set information apart from the main text. The rules for comma usage are complex and often difficult for young students to learn. The following list summarizes the most important comma usage rules:

- Commas are used to separate two independent clauses along with a coordinating conjunction.
  - George ordered the steak, but Bruce preferred the ham.
- Commas are used to separate coordinate adjectives.
  - She made herself a big bowl of cold, delicious ice cream.
- Commas are used to separate items in a series.
  - The list of groceries included cream, coffee, doughnuts, and tea.
- Commas are used to separate introductory words and phrases from the rest of the sentence.
  - For example, we have thirty students who demand a change.
- Commas are used to set off nonessential information and appositives.
  - Estelle, our newly elected chairperson, will be in attendance.
- Commas are used to set off the day and month of a date within a text.
  - I was born on February 16, 1958.
- Commas are used to set up numbers in a text of more than four digits.
  - We expect 25,000 visitors to the new museum.

Quotation marks have a number of different purposes. They enclose titles of short (or relatively short) literary works, such as short stories, chapters, and poems. (The titles of longer works, such as novels and anthologies, are italicized.) Additionally, quotation marks are used to enclose direct quotations within the text of a document where the quotation is integrated into the text. Writers also use quotation marks to set off dialogue:

- We will be reading the poem "Bright Star" in class today.
- The poem opens with the line "Bright star, would I were steadfast as thou art."

Apostrophes, sometimes referred to as single quotation marks, have several different purposes:

- They show possession: boy's watch, John and Mary's house
- They replace missing letters, numerals, and signs: do not = don't; 1989 = '89
- In certain instances, they are added to create plurals of letters, numerals, and signs in order to prevent confusion (e.g., "Capitalize I's in sentences.").

The following are less commonly used punctuation marks:

- **en dash (–):** indicates a range
- **em dash (—):** shows an abrupt break in a sentence and emphasizes the words within the em dashes
- **parentheses ( ):** enclose nonessential information
- **brackets [ ]:** enclose added words to a quotation and add insignificant information within parentheses
- **slash (/):** separates lines of poetry within a text or indicates interchangeable terminology
- **ellipses (…):** create a reflective pause or indicate that information has been removed from a quotation

Practice Questions

6) Which sentence includes an improperly placed comma?

   A. Ella, Cassie, and Cameron drove to South Carolina together.

   B. Trying to impress his friends, Carl ended up totaling his car.

   C. Ice cream is my favorite food, it is so cold and creamy.

   D. Mowing the lawn, Frank discovered a family of baby rabbits.

7) Which answer option would correct the punctuation in the following sentence?

Oak trees—with proper care—can grow upwards of thirty feet; providing shade for people, shelter for animals, and perches for birds.

   A. replace the em dashes with commas

   B. remove the comma after *people*

   C. insert an apostrophe at the end of *animals*

   D. replace the semicolon with a comma

Capitalization

Capitalization means writing the first letter of a word in uppercase and the remaining letters in lowercase. Capitalization is used in three main contexts:

- The first, and most common, context is in the first word after a period or the first word of a text. (E.g., The first word in each sentence of the paragraphs in this chapter is capitalized.)

- The second most common usage of capitalization is for proper nouns or adjectives derived from proper nouns. For instance, *France*—as the name of a country—is capitalized. Similarly, *French*—the adjective derived from the proper noun *France*—is also capitalized. The exception to this rule is when the adjective takes on a meaning that is independent of the original proper noun. (E.g., The term *french fries* is not capitalized.)

- The third usage of capitalization is in a title or honorific that appears before a name. For example: "**P**resident George Washington never lived in the capital." If, however, that same title is used *instead of* the name, or if the name and title are separated by a comma, it remains lowercase. For example, "The first **p**resident, George Washington, never lived in the capital" or "The **p**resident did not originally live in the capital."

Practice Question

8) Which sentence CORRECTLY uses capitalization?
   A. Robert and Kelly raced across the River in their small boats.
   B. ducks flying in a V-formation cross the Midwest in the fall.
   C. The chairman of the board, Jessica Smith, will lead today's meeting.
   D. The Senators from Virginia and Louisiana strongly favor the bill.

Mechanics Instruction

Mechanics instruction used to focus on drills, and many students did not understand the connection between the explicit study of grammatical conventions and their own writing. In recent years, however, most classrooms use a more integrated, or holistic, approach where mechanics and writing are taught together.

Many teachers and contemporary educational publishers focus on how a certain grammatical convention conveys a message in a particular way instead of focusing on the structure of language in isolation, which is not as helpful and may hinder oral and written language development. For example, capitalization and punctuation may not be necessary or appropriate when texting; however, in a formal expository essay for an academic audience, attention to these details is essential.

Furthermore, correct punctuation helps readers follow a writer's message and clearly see the relationships between ideas. For instance, short, choppy sentences structured in a nearly identical way may not appeal to or interest certain audiences. The following list describes some best practices and instructional techniques for teaching mechanics in context:

- **Writing workshop** is an organizational framework for teaching the writing process that includes a mini-lesson, work time, and share time. The mini-lesson can provide mechanics instruction for students to incorporate into their writing.

- **Targeted mechanics instruction** can be used with an individual student or at the class level. For example, after grading a student-authored short story, a teacher may need to provide explicit instruction in apostrophe use as a targeted lesson to the entire class. Or perhaps a teacher notices that only one or two students are struggling with the correct use of apostrophes. The teacher could then provide individualized instruction, perhaps through published exercises in a text or on a digital platform.

- Teachers can use **mentor texts** to teach grammar. Mentor texts describe high-quality writing (often published) that students can emulate in their own writing. These types of texts can be used to teach punctuation, capitalization, dialogue, sentence structure, style, format, and appropriateness to audience.

- Teachers can give students **writing assignments** to practice and demonstrate understanding of key components of mechanics. For example, students can write a paragraph with two compound sentences and two complex sentences or an essay in which they identify and circle all of the object or subject pronouns they used.

Practice Question

9) Why is focusing on how grammatical conventions convey messages in particular ways more helpful than focusing on the structure of language alone?

   A. because students may not be able to understand both concepts at once

   B. because students need to know how to determine the appropriate language to use based on context

   C. because understanding language structure is no longer critical in the modern world

   D. because students will need to rely less on language structure and more on grammatical conventions as their education continues

Form and Functions of Language

In addition to understanding the meaning and structure of words, students must also understand how words interact with each other and the content around them. The **function** of language is how it is used. Students must be able to determine the appropriate language for various academic contexts. For example, students correctly use language to describe a process, and adapt their language as needed to compare or contrast ideas. They should also be able to determine the appropriate level of formality in their language for different academic situations (e.g., an expository essay versus a personal narrative). When reading, students should be able to analyze how various English dialects and registers are used within and across different texts.

As students progress, they become able to intentionally select words, phrases, and punctuation for specific and precise purposes. For example, when writing a persuasive essay, students should know how to convey opinions using strong words:

- "Using cars as the primary mode of transportation is <u>harmful</u> to society in <u>every</u> way. Having too many cars on the roads causes pollution, noise, and lowers the quality of life. Taking public transportation benefits the environment and the community."

In the above sentence, *harmful* clearly has a negative connotation. The word *every* is an absolute word, leaving no room for nuance or argument in favor of cars.

However, when writing a description that compares objects or ideas, students would use more neutral language:

- *In some cities, cars are the main mode of transportation. In other cities, most people use public transportation.*

This sentence lacks powerful adjectives that carry any extreme connotations. It also lacks absolute words like *every, always,* or *never*.

<table>
<tr><td>

Check for Understanding:

Identify the language function and at least one language form in this sentence: "Pascal and Paul, you must try this new frozen yogurt immediately: it's the best!"
</td></tr>
</table>

While the functions of language refer to the ways in which students use language, the **form** of language refers to the structures that support those specific functions. Understanding form includes understanding the internal grammatical structure of words and specific phrases. For example, a student should understand the different ways in which words can be made singular or plural: *shoe* versus *shoes, goose* versus *geese,* and *deer* versus *deer*. Conjugating verbs is another example.

When learning language form, students must also identify cross-curricular vocabulary related to specific academic processes. These are words and phrases—verbs, complex prepositions, and nouns—used in a variety of different content areas: *hypothesize, in contrast to, analyze,* and so on.

As students master both language functions and form, they should be able to better manipulate words and phrases in order to communicate more clearly. This includes making informed choices in expanding, reducing, or combining sentences to increase the meaning of their writing, add interest, or introduce a specific style.

Practice Question

10) Which of the following is an example of a function of language?

A. identifying prepositional phrases

B. using descriptive adjectives

C. asking clarifying questions

D. mastering compound subjects

Discussion and Collaboration

Learning is a social construct; social learning tools like collaboration and discussion are important to student learning. Discussion should be regularly incorporated into the curriculum from the earliest years.

The goals of discussion are twofold: to construct student understanding of content and to develop communication skills. To begin, teachers should explicitly teach students the elements of a good discussion. An essential skill is **active listening:** the process of demonstrating engagement through positive body language and then paraphrasing or summarizing of the speaker's content. Other discussion skills include active participation, asking clarifying questions, constructive disagreement, seeking out all voices, and supporting arguments with evidence.

Once parameters have been established, the teacher should lead the students in a discussion. In one tactic, **immersion,** the teacher involves all students in a discussion with little redirection or guidance. In contrast, in **a fishbowl** a small subset of students engages in discussion while the remaining students watch. In either case, the discussion should be followed by reflection, allowing students to analyze what

was successful and unsuccessful about the discussion, and to find ways to improve their discussions in the future.

It is essential that teachers provide students ample opportunity to practice discussion, always followed by reflection. Through this process, students will learn to be respectful and considerate of others, to clearly express their own ideas orally, to listen and respond to the ideas of others, to ask clarifying questions and build on outside ideas, and to incorporate new ideas and perspectives into their own understanding.

The second form of social learning is **collaborative learning**. It is based on four general principles:

1. Students must be at the center of instruction.

2. Students learn more by working in groups.

3. Learning should focus on doing and interacting.

4. Students retain more information and gain more skills when addressing real-world problems.

Collaborative learning can take the form of peer learning or group learning. In **peer learning**, pairs or small groups of students discuss concepts or develop solutions to problems related to the content. With this method, students learn from each other, dispelling misconceptions and addressing misunderstandings. Informal practices include pair-share and talk-and-turns. More formal practices include case studies and debates. Many of the skills honed by discussions are also addressed in peer learning. Students must listen to each other, ask clarifying questions, and show mutual respect.

In **collaborative group work**, students typically work in larger groups or over a longer period of time. This approach is most often used with long-term projects in which students develop or pursue a particular question or problem, and then—working mostly independently of the teacher—gather the needed information to solve it. For example, in a unit on the environment and sustainability, the teacher might ask students to work in groups to reduce the classroom's energy use or waste creation. Students would then engage in research, develop plans, and test ideas, all working together.

By allowing students to work together to *do*, the teacher promotes important academic skills: formulating and answering questions, seeking help when needed, gathering and processing information, and evaluating and reflecting on the perspectives of others. Through this process, students develop self-management, oral communication, and leadership skills, as well as improve their understanding of the content.

In addition, collaborative learning builds student self-confidence, encouraging students to challenge themselves and to take greater risks. It prepares them for life beyond the classroom as they learn to navigate the challenges of working with others and to leverage the benefits of multiple minds.

Practice Question

11) Which of the following best explains the primary purpose of a fishbowl activity?

    A. to assess individual student understanding after a group project

    B. to allow students to observe and evaluate a discussion

    C. to encourage students to collaborate in addressing misconceptions about an idea

    D. to model for students how to develop effective discussion questions

Answer Key

1) C: Once speech becomes fully developed and students are generating their own sentences and paragraphs, basic rules of grammar can be introduced.

2) A: "While they read the paper" is a dependent clause; the subordinating conjunction *while* connects it to the independent clause "Anne and Peter drank their coffee languidly."

3) C: *Package* is the direct object of the verb *brought*.

4) D: The phrase is a verbal phrase modifying the noun *David*. It begins with the word *smelling*, derived from the verb *to smell*.

5) B: "Alligators . . . still" and "they . . . speed" are two independent clauses connected by a comma and the coordinating conjunction *but*.

6) C: "Ice cream . . . food" and "it . . . creamy" are two independent clauses. The writer should include a coordinating conjunction like *for* or separate the clauses with a semicolon instead of using a comma.

7) D: "Providing shade..." is not an independent clause; therefore it cannot be preceded by a semicolon.

8) C: *Jessica Smith*, as a proper noun, should be capitalized, but "chairman of the board" should not be capitalized because it is separated from the name by a comma.

9) B: Focusing solely on the structure of language in isolation is not helpful in real-world contexts (e.g., text messaging) and could even hinder oral or written language development in students.

10) C: A clarifying question addresses the purpose of the words used.

11) B: In a fishbowl, half of the class observes only, allowing them to witness both positive and negative elements of a discussion.

5. Writing and Writing Development

Writing Skills and Reading Development

From a very young age, children understand that written language is a way to communicate. As they develop reading and writing skills, children learn that writing is a means to both express and receive information. When they produce writing, students are giving reading experiences to others. When they consume writing, students are engaged in their own reading experiences. Both reading and writing help students develop pre-reading skills, such as letter-sound correspondence and phonemic awareness. For example, a student who titles a drawing "M" to denote it as an image of her mother understands that the symbol "M" stands for the sound /m/ and is part of communicating the meaning of the word *mother*.

As students grow and develop more advanced literacy skills, writing-related activities, such as spelling practice, can increase reading comprehension. Students who are exposed to high-frequency words in spelling or writing practice activities will strengthen their knowledge of these words. Since word identification skills are strongly linked to reading fluency, writing activities should be integrated with reading instruction and activities as much as possible.

Some theorists believe reading and writing are so interconnected that one cannot occur without the other. Even when students lack the motor skills to write themselves, many educators believe that writing can—and should—still be a meaningful part of literacy instruction.

One strategy that illustrates this belief is the **Language Experience Approach (LEA)**. With this approach, learners and teachers have a shared experience first. For example, they may visit the school garden as a class. Teachers or students then document the shared experience, usually with photographs. Students refer to the photographs when writing about the experience. With scaffolding from the teacher as necessary, students create a text about the shared experience. They then read the story aloud (with scaffolding as appropriate), noting any needed revisions. The final story is read aloud again, often accompanied by teacher-directed comprehension questions.

LEA helps students connect writing and reading because they are involved in both the creation of written language to communicate an experience and the reading of the written language that is used to communicate what happened.

Practice Question

1) Why should preschool children be encouraged to experiment with letters and text to label pictures they draw?

    A. because it strengthens receptive vocabulary

    B. because it helps develop gross motor skills

    C. because it contributes to an understanding of text as meaning

    D. because it encourages the transition from artistic to written expression

Developmental Stages of Writing

A child's journey to writing happens in phases and is influenced by encouragement from parents, teachers, and caretakers. **Writing development** involves three areas:

1. Conceptual knowledge (understanding the purpose of writing)

2. Procedural knowledge (understanding how to form letters and words)

3. Generative knowledge (using words to communicate meaning)

Even children as young as age two begin to draw pictures that they can use to communicate ideas. These images are their first written representations. Drawing develops into **scribbling**, which looks like letters. Wavy scribbling or mock handwriting may appear as children are exposed to print-rich home environments and classrooms. This is followed by forms that look like individual letters and then forms with actual letters that resemble individual words strung together.

In the **transitional writing stage**, children begin writing letters separated by spaces, although real words are generally not yet being formed. Even in the transitional writing stage, however, many children successfully copy letters and words from environmental sources. Writing a child's name or the name of a common classroom object on a card for a child to copy can encourage transitional writing. Teachers must remember that writing is still an emergent skill in children, and they therefore may invert letters or fail to accurately copy letters.

Table 5.1 Stages of Emergent Writing

Stage	Example
Drawing	

Table 5.1 Stages of Emergent Writing

Stage	Example
Scribbling	
Wavy Scribbles	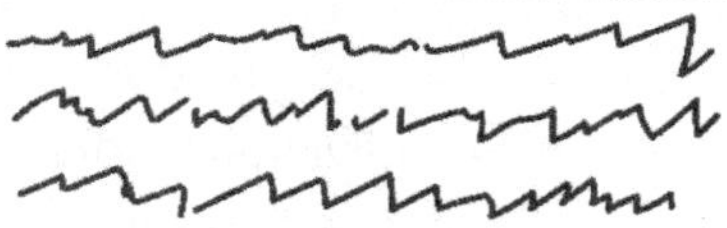
Letter-like Forms	
Letter Strings	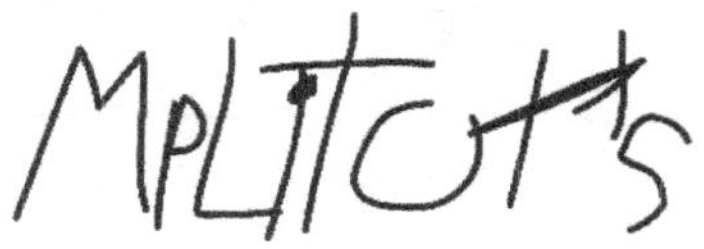
Transitional Writing	
Invented and Phonetic Spelling	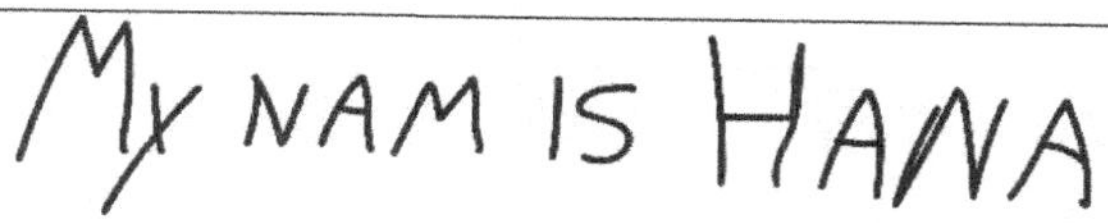 MY NAM IS HANA
Word and Phrase Writing	 DOG PIG
Conventional Spelling and Sentences	 HANNAH

As children learn sounds, they begin a phase of **invented spelling**. They start communicating words and ideas more clearly, though many words may have only beginning and ending sounds. This stage is a natural part of the process of emergent writing. Children should be allowed to express ideas and practice writing without an overemphasis on spelling errors. Explicit spelling instruction will generally begin in the

early elementary grades. Students will have plenty of time and practice to master these skills when they are developmentally ready to do so.

As children gain more knowledge of sounds and words, they will begin writing whole words, first with single letter-sound constructions, such as "dog," "hat," and "fun." This progresses to the correct spelling of more words and eventually to stringing together words to make phrases and short sentences.

It is important to see writing as a process and recognize that it can be affected by many factors. For example, students with conditions that impact fine motor skills functioning or young children with developmental delays in associated domains may have difficulty learning to write fluently. Expectations should be tailored to the individual student. Teachers should encourage and praise efforts rather than results while young people are developing these skills. Students typically go through ten developmental stages of writing; these are described in Table 5.2.

Table 5.2. Developmental Stages of Writing		
Stage	**Age**	**Student Milestones in this Stage**
Preconventional	3 – 5	• have awareness that print conveys meaning, but also have reliance on pictures to communicate visually • can include recognizable shapes and letters on drawings • can describe the significance of the objects in their drawings
Emerging	4 – 6	• use pictures when drawing, but may also label objects • can match some letters to sounds • can copy print they see in their environments
Developing	5 – 7	• can write sentences and no longer rely mainly on pictures • make attempts to use punctuation and capitalization • can spell words based on sound
Beginning	6 – 8	• can write several related sentences on a topic • can use word spacing, punctuation, and capitalization correctly • can create writing that others can read

Table 5.2. Developmental Stages of Writing		
Stage	**Age**	**Student Milestones in this Stage**
Expanding	7 – 9	▪ can organize sentences logically and use more complex sentence structures ▪ can spell high-frequency words correctly ▪ can respond to guidance and criticism from others
Bridging	8 – 10	▪ can use a clear beginning, middle, and end to write about a topic ▪ can begin to use paragraphs ▪ can consult outside resources (e.g., dictionaries)
Fluent	9 – 11	▪ can write both fiction and nonfiction with guidance ▪ can experiment with sentence length and complexity ▪ can edit for punctuation, spelling, and grammar.
Proficient	10 – 13	▪ can write well-developed fiction and nonfiction ▪ can use transitional sentences and descriptive language ▪ can edit for organization and style
Connecting	11 – 14	▪ can write in a number of different genres ▪ can develop a personal voice when writing ▪ can use complex punctuation
Independent	13 and older	▪ can explore topics in depth in fiction and nonfiction ▪ can incorporate literary devices in their writing ▪ can revise writing through multiple drafts

In elementary school, students learn how to write in a variety of genres:

- personal narrative
- tall tales
- correspondence
- poetry
- science fiction

- short stories
- essays
- research papers

Students also learn how to write using a variety of styles:

- descriptive
- narrative
- expository
- persuasive

Teachers select writing tasks that correlate with the content knowledge goals assigned to grade levels through district and state standards.

Students should understand that writing is a process and that even professional writers put their work through several phases before releasing the finished product. A **recursive writing process** means that writers may return to a previously completed part of the process. Also known as the **authoring cycle**, this process includes several phases in which ideas are transformed into written form to effectively communicate meaning:

- plan
- draft
- revise
- edit
- publish

The first step in planning is to **brainstorm** ideas, which can take many forms. One example is for teachers to prompt the class to generate ideas for topics and write them on the board or screen. Students can then create their own **webs** or **outlines** to organize these ideas.

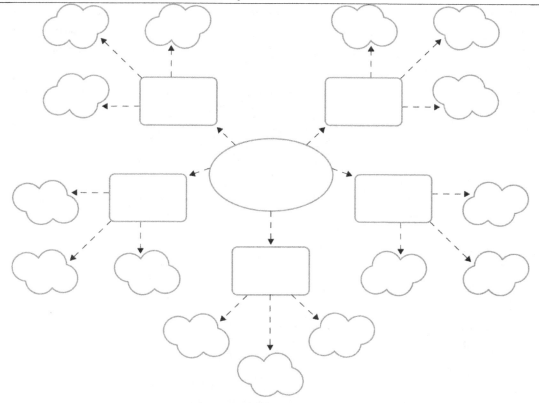

Figure 5.1. Brainstorming Web

This initial planning can help students organize the overall point and supporting details of their written works. These activities can be based on a book the students have read, their opinions of the work (e.g., "I liked the book," "I did not like the book," "My favorite/least favorite part was . . ."), and reasons for those opinions. Students might also write simple expository pieces that introduce a topic and then use supporting details to inform the reader.

Brainstorming activities can also help students organize the events they want to describe when writing narratives. As students move upward through the grades, writing assignments become more structured, and students learn the characteristics and conventions of writing using different forms, structures, and literary devices.

As with reading comprehension, teachers use a number of strategies and tools to guide students as they work to attain writing proficiency. **Graphic organizers** provide ways for students to organize their ideas and clarify thinking at the beginning of the writing process. Some examples include the following:

- **concept map:** Using boxes and/or circles and lines, students begin with a main idea and draw links to supporting ideas, adding additional links and cross-links as necessary.
- **story map:** Students brainstorm story elements and plan out the plot development of a story.
- **lists:** Students brainstorm writing topics, story ideas, sensory words, rhyming words, alliterative words, etc.
- **outlines:** Students create and revise formal working outlines as guides to writing expository essays and research papers.

- **sequence maps:** Students draw or write events in the order in which they will occur in a text.
- **beginning, middle, and end organizers:** Students plan the main structure of a writing piece by noting how it will begin (introduction), what is needed in the middle (body), and how it will end (conclusion).

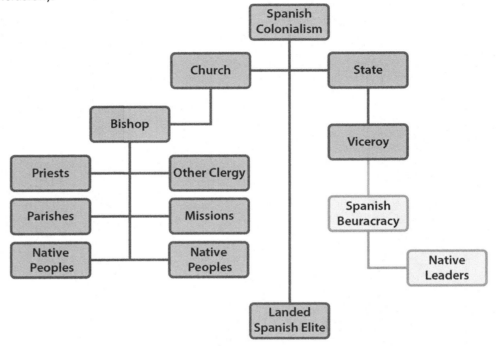

Figure 5.2. Concept Map

After brainstorming, students **draft** their individual pieces of writing and connect their ideas with an introductory statement, support, and concluding section. With scaffolding, students then go through a **revision** process where they address weaknesses in the writing. For example, they may need to add more supporting details or connecting words (*because*, *also*, *then*) to improve clarity. They can then **edit** for capitalization, end marks, and spelling.

Teachers can help students during the revision process by giving them a simple checklist to help ensure they have met certain criteria. One such checklist is the **COPS mnemonic:** capitalization, organization, punctuation, and spelling.

Teachers can also use peer and teacher feedback as part of the revision process. Receiving feedback helps students understand that the main purpose of writing is to communicate ideas, so having other readers offer their perceptions and suggestions is an important part of revision.

Students should **publish** their works after the final copies are created, particularly if the writing projects are significant in scope. Having students read their works aloud is one simple and immediate way to publish (as well as a way to link reading and writing), as is posting student work on classroom or school

bulletin boards. Teachers may have students organize and bind their works into simple books with string or brads, or they may collect student works and create class-wide literary samplers.

If a teacher uses student portfolios in the classroom, students can prepare their pieces for inclusion in digital or physical folders. This may involve transcribing the piece digitally, adding illustrations, or matting it on construction paper. Teachers should also emphasize that sharing work with others is an important part of publishing. This is a great way to build a home–school connection while encouraging students to share their work with parents. Teachers should also show student work samples or portfolios at parent conferences to further build the home–school connection.

Practice Question

2) A sixth-grade teacher sponsors a creative writing club that meets weekly after school. He is looking for a high-impact way to publish student work and share it with the school community. What is the BEST way to accomplish this?

A. inviting administrators to attend one of the club meetings and listen to students read their work

B. encouraging students to read their pieces at home to their family members

C. planning a digital or print literary journal that can be shared across the school

D. teaching students to use publishing and graphic design software to format their pieces

---

Check for Understanding:

A student has completed a first draft of an essay about the novel *Roll of Thunder, Hear My Cry*. What should the teacher ask the student to do next?

In the earliest grades, elementary school students are provided with open-ended opportunities to develop as writers through both collaborative and independent writing activities such as lists, names, thematic vocabulary, pages for class books, individual books, journal entries, and responses to daily writing prompts. In addition, students practice forming letters using tactile and paper/pencil materials. **Writers' workshops**, in which students peer review, edit, and share writing, allow students to learn the writing process in small groups under a teacher's guidance.

Creative writing assignments provide opportunities for students to focus on concepts taught across the language arts curriculum. Reading and language concepts, such as figurative language and word choice, are naturally integrated into the writing process, as are literary elements such as character, setting, point of view, and plot.

In addition, **poetry** writing provides a wealth of opportunities for reinforcing concepts such as syllabification, spelling, vocabulary, parts of speech, and rhyming words. Some forms of poetry that may be accessible to students include the following:

- **cinquain:** a five-line poem with a 2–4–6–8–2 syllable pattern
- **haiku:** a three-line poem with a 5–7–5 syllable pattern

- **acrostic:** a poem written for each letter in a word or phrase, reflecting its meaning
- **diamante:** a seven-line diamond-shaped poem requiring different parts of speech on each line
- **quatrain:** a four-line stanza with a rhyme scheme

Practice Questions

3) Which of the following elements shapes each paragraph in a writing task?

    A. the thesis

    B. the topic sentence

    C. the drafting stage

    D. the outline

4) Which type of graphic organizer is depicted below?

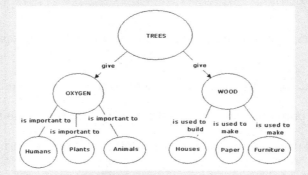

    A. outline

    B. story map

    C. beginning, middle, and end organizer

    D. concept map

Inquiry and Research

The Research Process

Teaching students how to do **research** and prepare reports based on that research is a fundamental role of language arts teachers. Beginning in the early grades, students learn how to use print and multimedia sources to find out information and develop presentations—visual, written, and spoken—to share what they learned. Students learn how to navigate text and digital features, formulate questions, locate information, evaluate sources for reliability, identify primary and secondary sources, take notes, and paraphrase to avoid plagiarism. The research process is approached in a series of clear, focused, and manageable steps over a specified duration.

As students grow as writers, they learn how to cite sources to support their ideas in research papers. The research paper is an expository essay that contains references to outside materials that legitimize claims made in the essay. In order to avoid **plagiarism**—the intentional copying and credit-taking of another person's work—students learn to **paraphrase** supporting information, or briefly restate the information in

their own words. They also learn to include **citations** that name original sources of new information and are taught how to differentiate between primary sources, secondary sources, reliable sources, and unreliable sources:

- **Primary sources** are original materials representative of an event, experience, place, or time period. They are direct or firsthand accounts in the form of text, image, record, sound, or item.

- **Secondary sources** inform about events, experiences, places, or time periods, but the information is provided by someone who was not directly involved and who used primary sources to discuss the material.

- **Reliable sources** are trustworthy materials that come from experts in the field of study.
  - These sources have **credibility** because they include extensive bibliographies listing the sources used to support the information provided.
  - Some examples of reliable sources are published books, articles in credible magazines, and research studies provided by educational institutions.

- **Unreliable sources** are untrustworthy materials from institutions or people who do not have the educational background, expertise, or evidence of legitimate sources to support their claims. Some examples of unreliable sources are self-published materials, studies done to sell products, and opinion pieces.

Research and library skills are important parts of developing overall student literacy. There are seven steps in the research process:

- **identifying and focusing on the topic:** This might be as simple as having students pick a topic they want to learn more about or asking students to develop a research question they wish to answer (before searching online).

- **finding background information and conducting a preliminary search:** This involves getting a general overview of a topic and possible subtopics. During this stage, students may use online search engines to learn about a particular topic.

- **locating materials:** This could involve work at the library and online. Teachers should encourage students to explore a wide variety of possible resources. Depending on the research topic, students should seek out primary sources, such as speeches or diaries, surveys or census data, photographs of an event, and several other media that give eyewitness accounts of an event. Many primary sources are available online, and many sites organize these sources into accessible formats for students. Many materials that students find will also be secondary sources. These include the majority of books, articles, and web pages devoted to a topic.

> **Did You Know?**
>
> Some state standards require students to know the differences between primary and secondary accounts, so this type of analysis should be part of the research process.

- **evaluating sources:** Students should determine if certain sources are useful and accessible to them. For example, a library database may generate results for articles in publications the library does not have. Some resources may be overly technical or written for older audiences. Students should also make sure they have credible sources written by experts.

This stage in the research process might also be a good time to introduce students to the different types of information available on the internet and the elements that make sources more reliable (listed authors, *.edu* or *.org* domains, publication dates, and so on).

- **note-taking:** Note-taking may involve the use of formal note cards or simply jotting down main ideas. Teachers should ensure that students understand the idea of paraphrasing as they take notes. Paraphrasing can help students prevent **plagiarizing**, or presenting someone else's words as their own. Instruction for note-taking should be carried out as developmentally appropriate per student age.

- **writing:** This includes organizing all the notes into sentences and paragraphs. Students should be aware of the overall organization of their work as they introduce a focused topic, provide support, and write a conclusion. Depending on the age group teachers work with, they may have students make posters to present their research instead of writing a formal papers.

> ### Did You Know?
>
> There are many intentionally fake sites on the internet designed to help students practice determining whether online information is legitimate. One example is found at https://zapatopi.net/treeoctopus, where students can learn about the Pacific Northwest tree octopus.

- **citing sources:** This may include creating in-text **citations** and preparing a **bibliography**. To simplify these elements for young students, teachers might have them simply list titles of books and authors. Students in the upper elementary grades can create more sophisticated bibliographies using Modern Language Association (MLA) style. MLA is generally regarded as the simplest citation style and the one to which students are first introduced.

The steps listed above can be simplified for very young students and varied as needed, depending on the scope of the research project. For example, kindergartners can gather information from sources to answer a simple research question, and first-grade students can contribute to a class-wide research project with teacher support. The key is to introduce students to the various parts of the research process while providing scaffolding as needed to support them as they explore new outlets for their developing literacy.

Practice Question

5) Which of the following is a primary source that is appropriate for a third-grade class to use as part of a research project?

A. a history journal article written at a 770 Lexile level by a noted WWII scholar

B. online photographs of soldiers taken during WWII

C. a documentary video about American pilots in WWII made by public television

D. transcripts of an interview with a WWII pilot at a 1400 Lexile level

Digital Tools

Increasingly, schools are using digital learning tools in their curricula. Many schools have one or more subscriptions to various educational technology platforms that may enhance student learning and **digital literacy**, which is defined as the ability to find, use, and create digital information. **Media literacy**, a key

part of digital literacy, describes the ability of students to access, analyze, evaluate, and communicate information in both digital and physical forms.

Some students may be experienced with accessing digital information at home on computers, tablets, or phones; however, not all students will have the same level of digital literacy. Teachers should explicitly instruct students about strategies for finding and assessing the usefulness of digital information. The internet has created an unlimited platform for disseminating information, and students must be taught early to not trust all sources and how to determine the validity and usefulness of sources.

Digital tools also enable students to differentiate literacy instruction through adaptive software programs that target practice for individual skill levels. Technological tools can also aid students with special needs or limited English proficiency through their daily activities in the classroom. Devices and applications that allow nonverbal children to communicate and those that help English language learners quickly translate new words may become indispensable learning aids.

Teachers should also incorporate digital tools into the writing process as appropriate. These may include word processing or presentation software to help students with drafting and revising, and digital storytelling sites, which help students create and publish visual stories. The classroom or school may have a website or social media page for publishing student-created content. Before publishing any student work online, however, teachers should always check with the school's administration and get parental consent.

6) A school's fourth-grade teacher is asked to incorporate more technology into his lessons in order to meet new district standards. The teacher did not grow up with technology and does not think his students need it. What is the MOST valid argument that can be made in favor of technology in order to help the teacher see its value?

    A. Students play video and computer games at home, so they should use technology at school too.

    B. Technology may help the teacher differentiate instruction for struggling readers.

    C. The district standards are always based on what is best for students, so he should heed them.

    D. Technology is not bad as long as it is strictly controlled by the teacher.

7) A teacher has just provided students with a general overview of a research project due at the end of the semester. Which of the following is MOST appropriate as a first task?

    A. to select a topic and locate some general information on it

    B. to develop an outline that lists the main idea and supporting details

    C. to choose reliable primary and secondary resources

    D. to formulate an appropriate research question on a topic

8) Which of the following is considered a reliable source for research about California?

    A. a personal blog about living in California

    B. a research paper published by the state of California

    C. an advertisement for California real estate

    D. a letter to the editor about California roadways

Presentation of Knowledge and Ideas

Listening and speaking are the pathways to literacy. Children typically enter elementary school with an ability to orally communicate ideas, experiences, and concepts. The role of teachers is to help students hone these skills for academic and social growth.

Students learn strategies for listening and speaking that enhance their abilities to listen carefully, think critically, identify relevant information, articulate clearly, and use appropriate vocal cues and word choices. Students are tasked with communicating for a variety of purposes, audiences, and contexts and have opportunities to engage in active listening during discussions of text, topics, and community.

Students in elementary school also learn how to prepare and engage in small-group and individual oral presentations. They learn how to organize the information they want to present as well as techniques for presenting the information in ways that capture and maintain the attention of the audience. The following oral presentation skills provide an overview of what elementary school students need to know in order to effectively communicate with their audiences:

> **Helpful Hint:**
>
> The organization of an oral presentation follows the same structure as that of a written essay: introduction, body, and conclusion. Similarly, the graphic organizers associated with writing can be used to develop oral presentations.

- **delivery:** posture, articulation, intonation, volume, eye contact, and expression
- **organization:** a logical presentation structure with the following components:
  - a brief, attention-grabbing hook that captures the audience's interest (e.g., an amusing thought, an interesting prop, an intriguing fact, or a thought-provoking statement)
  - an introduction that states the topic and gives a brief overview of what will be covered
  - a body of supporting evidence and/or details that correlate to and support the topic
  - a conclusion that summarizes the presentation's main points
- **audience awareness:** preparedness, appropriateness, and ability to hold audience attention
- **visuals and/or audio:** supporting materials that reinforce content such as props, posters, digital media, photographs, and music
- **collaboration:** creative, cohesive, and logical group presentations

Students are provided with opportunities to strengthen listening skills during classmates' oral presentations. They are tasked with providing **constructive feedback**—positively worded suggestions—derived from the criteria for active listening: focus, respect, objectivity, and paraphrasing.

Practice Questions

9) Students have been placed in small groups to prepare theater presentations that they will perform for each other. How might each group BEST meet the needs of its audience?

    A. by reciting their lines in quiet voices during the performance

    B. by passing around a script to read from during the performance

    C. by using classroom materials as props during the performance

    D. by skipping some parts of the story during the performance

10) Mr. Couch has his students take turns doing show-and-tell presentations every Friday afternoon. Which of the following is a PRIMARY benefit of show-and-tell opportunities for students?

    A. Students make decisions about what to share.

    B. Students rest at the end of a busy week.

    C. Students practice speaking in front of an audience.

    D. Students are rewarded for doing their homework.

Principles of Effective Writing

As students become more proficient writers, which will involve revising and examining their own writing and the writing of others, they should be mindful of what makes written communication effective. Successful writing has a central **focus**, or main idea (often referred to as a **central idea** in state and national standards). Brainstorming and other prewriting activities can help students maintain focus as they plan a piece. While students will mainly be exposed to professional writing that has already been edited, having them identify the author's focus across a broad range of texts will increase reading and writing capabilities.

Additionally, students should identify how the author uses details, examples, and other elements as part of overall concept development. They should be critical of how authors support their arguments and determine whether the evidence is sufficient. Students can then use these skills to critically reflect on their own writing and decide whether they have adequately proven a point.

> **Did You Know?**
>
> Having effective writing skills is a key component of success in higher education. Students who must take remedial or developmental college courses in writing and/or math (estimated at 40 – 60 percent) are less likely to complete their degree program on time or at all.

A knowledge of basic text **organization** will also help students become critical readers and effective writers. While there are many ways to organize and structure text, most effective writing has an **introduction**, several supporting details organized in a logical sequence, and a **conclusion** that wraps up the focus of the piece. It is helpful to have students practice labeling these parts in various texts. But even very young children can understand the idea of text organization by being shown the beginning, middle, and end of a story. As students edit and revise their work, they should organize their ideas so that the reader can follow the information in a logical pattern.

Each piece of writing also has a unique **style**, or approach. Style can describe the author's choice of words. It also includes sentence and paragraph structure. Both word choice and structure can make a piece **formal**, **informal**, or somewhere in between. Additionally, all written work has a **tone**, or attitude, that the author takes toward a subject or audience. A writer's tone might be hopeful, sarcastic, pessimistic, etc.

One part of selecting a style and tone is the intended purpose and audience. Students should pay attention to the audiences of their written works. A formal style is appropriate for writing a letter to the principal asking for a longer recess. A note to a friend, however, would probably be written in an informal

style. When reading any text, students should consider why an author chose a particular style convention or tone:

- Did the writer intend to argue a point to a hostile audience?
- Did the writer have a goal of informing a group of students about the differences between income and expenses?
- Did the author use a formal or informal style?

Mechanics are the structural elements of writing and include punctuation, capitalization, spelling, grammar, and general conventions of usage. Like most procedural knowledge of writing, this proficiency may vary among students and grade levels. A kindergarten class, for example, may be focused on a unit about capitalizing the letter *I*, whereas a second-grade class may be working on forming the past tense of verbs.

Teachers should not presume knowledge of English language conventions among students whose first language is not English. The correct use of prepositions, irregular verbs, and pronouns may be particularly challenging for these students until they get more experience with common usage patterns. Teachers should always aim for growth—not perfection—when helping students develop skills to edit their writing for errors in mechanics. These skills continue to build throughout a student's schooling.

Practice Question

11) A sixth-grade teacher is developing a rubric to score student writing. Which of the following categories would appear on the rubric under the heading of "mechanics"?

A. word choice

B. style

C. punctuation

D. tone

Instructional Strategies for Developing Writing Skills

Teachers can use many strategies and activities to help students develop strong writing skills throughout the writing process.

Planning

Data dump is an informal prewriting method whereby students write down a topic and then any words that immediately come to mind. For example, a student might write the word *environmentalism* and then list the terms *climate change, pollution,* and *endangered animals*. After a data dump, students select only the words that most closely pertain to their chosen topics.

In **guided prewriting**, the class or group of students comes up with ideas and/or a writing structure. The teacher helps by visually projecting ideas or writing them on a board. Mapping, outlining, webbing, and listing are common strategies for guided prewriting.

RAFT is a prewriting method that encourages students to consider their purpose, audience, and organization pattern. Students think about the following questions:

- **the role of the writer:** What perspective will you, as the writer, take?
- **the audience:** Who will read the piece?
- **the format:** How will you, the writer, communicate your message (e.g., story, essay, drama)?
- **the topic:** What will you write about?

Media or tech-enabled planning involves students watching a video, looking at images, or searching for ideas online. These can be useful strategies for students who are stuck or who do not have an opinion on an issue or a clear topic about which to write.

Practice Question

12) What does the RAFT method aim to encourage students to consider when writing?

    A. reason for writing, audience, finalization process, and topic

    B. role of the writer, audience, format, and topic

    C. role of the writer, audience, format, and task of the writer

    D. reason for writing, annotation, format, and topic

Drafting

Framed paragraphs are a scaffolding technique to help students write paragraphs. Framed paragraphs are fill-in-the-blank templates that students use to write their own paragraphs. For example, an "empty" frame for a persuasive paragraph might look like the following:

I think that _____. The first reason I think this is because_____. The second reason I think this is because_____. Lastly, I believe that_____. For these reasons, _____should_____.

Paragraph hamburgers (i.e., **essay hamburgers**) encourage students to plan a paragraph or essay with the topic sentence or introduction as the top "bun" and the concluding sentence or concluding paragraph as the bottom "bun." The supporting details or body paragraph are the middle parts of the "hamburger."

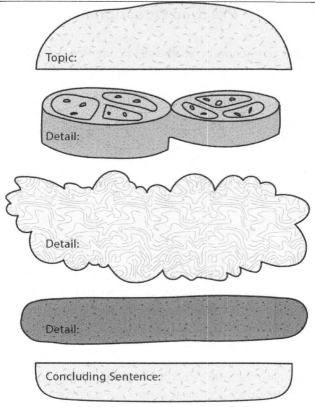

Figure 5.3. Paragraph Hamburger

Shared or interactive writing is a process whereby writers are scaffolded by "experts," usually teachers:

- In **shared writing**, the teacher scribes for the students, who must give explicit instructions on what to write. This can be an effective method for students who have difficulty with the physical task of writing.
- In **interactive writing**, students compose the written piece, but the teacher serves as the subject matter expert who facilitates the process.

In both methods, the teacher helps scaffold learning as needed. This might involve asking leading questions ("What should happen after_____?"), providing ideas for transitions or breaks ("Let's start our next sentence with 'Additionally . . .'"), or even providing more explicit instruction to reinforce concepts ("Now, we need to add supporting details. What supporting details can we add?"). Shared or interactive writing helps students see and participate in effective models for writing, which can give them confidence and strategies to use in independent writing assignments.

Practice Question

13) A third-grade teacher wants to encourage students to organize their thoughts into coherent paragraphs. Which of the following instructional strategies BEST meets this goal?

    A. data dump

    B. self-assessment

    C. hamburger method

    D. COPS mnemonic

Revision and Editing

Modeling or think-alouds can be used with sample pieces. These can be teacher- or student-authored pieces (with student permission and names removed as requested) but should involve whole-class input. The pieces can be projected on a screen and edited through a "track changes" feature in a word-processing program or even copied onto a transparency and written on. This process is helpful since it allows students to participate in and experience the revision and editing processes. Teachers can encourage input from the class and model strategies to revise writing, such as reading aloud and identifying and refining thesis and topic sentences.

Conferencing or peer review can also be used after first modeling the process and providing guidelines to students. Research proves that the most successful writing conferences are structured and occur when students have a clear idea of what type of feedback they should provide and how to give feedback in a constructive way.

Self-assessment should also be taught as part of the revision process. Students can be given a checklist or rubric from which to assess their own drafts and make necessary revisions.

Practice Question

14) Which of the following would NOT help students participating in a peer review?

    A. providing examples of successful peer review approaches

    B. modeling the process with the students ahead of time

    C. offering the students a free-choice approach to providing feedback

    D. giving students a checklist of items on which to provide feedback

Answer Key

1) D: This is a great first step in helping students begin to write.

2) C: A school-wide literary journal is an effective way to publish and distribute creative writing in a high school.

3) B: The topic sentence for each paragraph introduces the idea that the paragraph will discuss

4) D: A concept map shows the relationship between topics and subtopics, as in the hierarchy portrayed in the image in this question

5) B: This is a primary source that is easily accessible to third-grade students.

6) B: This is one benefit that may help his students and that he might have a hard time arguing against.

7) A: The first step in any research project is to select a topic of interest and acquire background knowledge about it. Once general information on a topic is understood, a relevant research question can be formulated

8) B: A study published by a government institution is a reliable research source.

9) C: Props add interesting visuals to a performance and reinforce comprehension.

10) C: Opportunities for show-and-tell provide students with practice speaking in front of an audience. The audience members also receive practice exercising their active listening skills.

11) C: Punctuation is a major part of the mechanics of writing.

12) A: RAFT is a prewriting method that encourages students to consider their purpose, audience, and organization pattern. Students think about the following: the role of the writer, the audience, the format, and the topic.

13) C: Paragraph hamburgers (i.e., **essay hamburgers**) encourage students to plan a paragraph or essay with the topic sentence or introduction as the top "bun" and the concluding sentence or concluding paragraph as the bottom "bun." The supporting details or body paragraph are the middle parts of the "hamburger."

14) C: Constructive feedback is a critical component to a successful peer review process, and knowing how to provide constructive feedback is an important skill for students to learn; offering students a free-choice approach to providing feedback to their peers is therefore not helpful in this situation.

6. Literary Genres and Text Types

Literary Genres

Literature can be classified into **genres**, which are categories of works that are similar in format, content, tone, or length. Most works fall into one of four broad literary genres:

- nonfiction
- fiction
- drama
- poetry

As students experience each genre throughout a school year, they should receive instruction that integrates all aspects of literacy. That is, students should not only experience reading practice in each genre, they should also have plenty of writing and discussion practice to deepen their knowledge of the genre they are studying.

Nonfiction

Nonfiction is a genre of prose writing that is defined by the use of information that is true and accurate to the best of the author's knowledge; however, this does not mean that nonfiction is dry or uninspiring. Nonfiction texts are written to inform, to reflect, and to entertain, and nonfiction writing comes in many forms, most of which display creativity and originality in how factual information is presented. One of the most common forms is **literary**, or **creative nonfiction**, which is a mix of expressive and informative writing that tells a true, verifiable, or documented story in a compelling, artistic way. Nonfiction has many components, which are discussed in a separate section later in this chapter.

Practice Question

1) Which of the following is NOT an example of nonfiction?
   A. an autobiography of Barack Obama
   B. a biography of George W. Bush
   C. the *Frog and Toad* series of books
   D. articles from *TweenTribune*

Fiction

Fiction is a prose genre that is made up of narratives whose details are not based in truth but are instead the author's creations. Students can be guided to determine whether a text is fiction or nonfiction by asking whether the text is a "true" or "real" story.

Fiction is typically written in the form of novels and short stories. Many subgenres fall under the category of fiction:

- **Folklore** is a set of beliefs and stories of a particular people and are passed down through the generations. It comes in many forms, including:
  - fables: short stories intended to teach moral lessons
  - fairy tales: stories that involve magical creatures such as elves and fairies
  - myths: stories, often involving gods or demigods, that attempt to explain certain practices or phenomena
  - legends: unverifiable stories that seem to have a degree of realism about them
  - tall tales: stories that are set in realistic settings but include characters with wildly exaggerated capabilities

Students can be guided to identify folklore by asking certain questions:

- Are there supernatural elements, such as magic, dragons, or fairies?
- Does the story teach a lesson?
- Do the characters in the stories have exaggerated abilities?
- Is the story from a particular cultural tradition?

Science fiction is a category of fiction in which writers tell imaginative stories that are grounded in scientific and technological theories or realities. Science fiction writing often explores ideas involving the future of humanity and its relationship with the universe or with technology. A subcategory of science fiction is **dystopian fiction**, in which authors explore social, cultural, and political structures in the context of a futuristic world.

Horror fiction is intended to frighten, startle, or disgust the reader. Horror fiction often involves paranormal or psychological content. **Mysteries** and **thrillers**, which may also arouse fear or paranoia, tend to be fast-paced and outcome-driven; they also tend to focus on human behaviors or relationships and not on paranormal activity.

Realistic fiction is meant to be relatable for readers. Authors of realistic fiction try to create a degree of verisimilitude in their writing, especially in the dialogue between characters. **Historical fiction** relies on realistic settings and characters from an earlier time to tell new stories. The setting is often central to the motivations and actions of characters. Students might need to explore the background of a historical era before they can comprehend a historical fiction text at the highest level.

Satire is a literary text that uses critical humor to reveal vice and foolishness in individuals and institutions. The purpose of satire is to somehow improve the object of ridicule. The literary or rhetorical devices that create satire include sarcasm, irony, mockery, exaggeration, and understatement as well as an honest narrative/speaking voice that is dismayed or appalled by the object of the satire. Because satire is a complex literary device that requires comprehension well beyond a literal or even basic inferential level, it is regarded as a more challenging type of text reserved for older students and more advanced readers.

Children's literature is a genre in its own right. It often includes **myths, legends,** or **folktales** written for a young audience. It tends to have characters who are children; if animals or mythical creatures are the characters, they tend to behave in the ways in which a child would. The genre also tends to focus on characters who learn an important lesson, often one that is applicable to life as a whole. Other characteristics of children's literature include accessible vocabulary and situations or events that children

can relate to and find appealing. Many children's books, even those for intermediate readers, often include vivid illustrations to help bring the plot to life.

Readers of all ages usually enjoy fiction texts, thanks to relatable characters and well-developed plots. Teachers often use familiar stories as springboards to more in-depth comprehension because students are familiar with the literal meaning of the text. For this reason, it is common to have many readings of the same story in an early childhood classroom.

Reading several interpretations of a familiar story, such as *Cinderella*, from different cultural perspectives can allow students to apply background knowledge of a familiar tale in new contexts. While there are many specific strategies to aid students in comprehension of literary texts, some of the most common include:

- storyboards and event sequence frames or timelines
- story maps (beginning, middle, end) or plot diagrams (rising action, climax, falling action, resolution)
- character maps (actions, feelings, appearance, dialogue)
- character trait identification charts

The **SQ3R strategy** was developed for reading textbooks, but it is useful for many different reading materials:

- **s**urvey: previewing the text and taking note of graphics, headings, etc.
- **q**uestion: generating questions about the text after previewing
- **r**ead: reading and looking for answers for the questions
- **r**ecite: rehearsing or saying the answers to the questions
- **r**eview: reviewing text and answering or responding to any other questions

With a **directed reading-thinking activity (DR-TA)**, students make predictions and read up to a preselected stopping point. They then evaluate and refine predictions based on text evidence.

The **QAR Strategy** encourages students to identify the type of question and to think about *how* to find the answer:

- "Right there" questions are literal questions that require only the location of the relevant part.
- "Think and search" questions require synthesis from multiple parts of the text.
- "Author and you" questions require the text to have been read, but the answer is not directly in the text. These are typically inference and depth of knowledge (DOK) 2 and 3 questions.
- "On my own" questions require background knowledge and do not rely on text evidence directly.

> **Think About It:**
>
> In selecting books and passages for curricular integration, which genres are most appropriate for social studies, music, or art?

Practice Question

2) A reading interventionist is working with a second-grade student receiving Tier 3 interventions in fluency and decoding. Before the day's activity, which will involve reading from a leveled reader, the interventionist asks the student to preview the booklet's title and illustrations and make a prediction about the type of book it is. What does this activity aim to help the student with?

 A. developing metacognition

 B. applying fix-up strategies

 C. determining genre

 D. analyzing plot

Drama

Drama is expressive writing that tells a story to an audience through the actions and dialogue of characters, which are brought to life by actors who play the roles on stage. Dramatic works, called **plays**, can be written in poetic or lyrical verse or in regular prose. Along with the **dialogue** between the characters, authors rely on **stage directions** to describe the sets and to give directions to the actors about what they are to do.

In **drama**, most of the story is centered around dialogue between characters. They are usually separated into segments (e.g., chapters known as **acts**) and smaller subsegments (generally with a consistent setting), known as **scenes**. In some plays, actors perform long speeches, known as **monologues**, in which the characters explain their thinking about philosophical ideas or social issues. These monologues can be directed toward another character. A monologue that delivered as if nobody were listening is called a **soliloquy** (as in Shakespeare's famous "To be or not to be" soliloquy from *Hamlet*). Sometimes characters in drama (or fiction) have very unique attributes, such as a manner of speech, dress, or a catchphrase. Such devices make characters memorable to readers and are known as **character tags**.

It is important to have older students think about how both stage directions and dialogue contribute to a play's meaning. To jog student interest, especially in linguistically complex dramas like those of Shakespeare, teachers might have students watch video clips of actual performances. Comparing specific scenes performed by different actors stimulates interest and can be used to discuss the different ways in which a scene can be interpreted.

Students may also benefit from acting out scenes or giving speeches, allowing them to express their own interpretations of the characters or action. To engage students in writing activities, a teacher may have them write their own scripts or write a research report on a play's context, author, characters, or subject matter.

Using drama in the classroom is a great way to get students interested in different types of texts. One idea includes setting up a simple **stage** in a kindergarten or elementary classroom as a natural outgrowth of a dramatic play center. When building on students' innate curiosity and imagination, the possibilities are endless. Acting out dramas not only helps students work on expressive reading (**prosody**), it also reinforces social and emotional learning as students analyze the emotions and actions of characters.

Practice Question

3) Drama is a genre well suited for helping students develop which of the following?

    A. phonemic awareness

    B. prosody

    C. alliteration

    D. concepts of print

Poetry

Poetry is imaginative, expressive verse writing that is characterized by rhythm, unified and concentrated thought, concrete images, specialized language, and the use of patterns. Different poetic forms utilize techniques and structures in unique ways.

A **line** is a unit of poetry. The lines of a poem can be separated by punctuation, meter, and/or rhyme. Although a line may be a unit of attention, it is usually not a unit of meaning.

A **stanza** is a group of lines followed by a space. Each stanza of a poem may have a specific number of lines; the lines are sometimes arranged in a pattern created by meter and/or a rhyme scheme. The pattern is often repeated in each stanza, although it can be varied for effect:

- A stanza with two lines is a **couplet**.
- A stanza with three lines is a **tercet**.
- A stanza with four lines is a **quatrain**.
- A stanza with five lines is a **cinquain**.

Modern poems may have stanzas with varying lengths or no stanzas at all. Some modern poems are written entirely in **free verse**, (i.e., without any fixed form).

While poetry may be associated with older children, even young students can appreciate and recognize **rhyme**. Students should be encouraged to recognize and create their own rhyming words as an additional outgrowth of phonological awareness. Asking students to name all the words they can think of that rhyme with *dog*, for example, will allow for continued practice with rhymes.

Meter—the rhythm, or beat, of the poem—can also be used to engage young students since a beat is something to which students can clap, stomp, or dance. Many timeless books for children, such as *One Fish, Two Fish, Red Fish, Blue Fish* and *Each Peach Pear Plum*, have both rhyme and meter, giving young children exposure to poetry.

Teachers can introduce several common types of poems to students during reading instruction:

- A **ballad** is a short, narrative song about an event that is considered important. Ballads are intended to be recited. They are characterized by a dramatic immediacy, focusing on one crucial situation or action that often leads to a catastrophe.
- A **sonnet** is a lyrical poem with fourteen lines, usually written in **iambic pentameter**, which is a pattern that alternates stressed and unstressed syllables in a line of verse with ten syllables per line.

- A **haiku** is a short poem format that originated in Japan. It has three lines of five, seven, and five syllables.
- A **villanelle** is usually nineteen lines long. It has five stanzas, each with three lines, and a final stanza of four lines. It includes a refrain—two lines that repeat throughout the poem and which follow a specific pattern.

Teachers can use poetry lessons to encourage students to consider the effect a poem has on them personally as well as the aesthetics of a poem itself. To introduce poetry and build interest for a poetry unit, a teacher might select an especially forceful poem, read it dramatically, and invite students to discuss their responses.

When students are analyzing a poem, it is important that they read it more than once. The teacher can model with a **think-aloud**, the process of modeling one's thinking during a reading. Students should have copies of poems to annotate and have a routine for collaborative and independent poetry reading. Examples of such routines include the following:

- an initial reading to experience the mood of the poem and the musicality of the language
- a second reading to focus on the pauses and thought units and to identify the **speaker**, who may not be the same person as the poet
- a third, close reading to take marginal notes on the structure of the poem, the denotation (literal meaning) and connotations (subtle meanings) of unfamiliar words, the impact of imagery and figurative language, and the meaning of confusing lines or phrases
- a final reading to produce some thematic ideas, drawn from the details

Along with analyzing poems, students can present their original poetry in classroom "coffee houses" or "poetry slams."

Poetry often uses **figurative language**, or phrases not meant to be interpreted literally:

- A **simile** compares two things of a different type ("brave like a lion").

- A **metaphor** applies a characteristic or meaning to an object or action that is not literally applicable ("the anger of the rose stung us with its sharp fury").

> **Check Your Understanding:**
>
> Lexile text measures are not used for poetry. Create a list of qualitative text features that could determine the appropriateness of a poem for a grade level or group of students.

Poems may also use **sensory imagery**, or descriptive language that appeals to one of the five senses ("the shrill cry of the alarm").

Practice Question

4) A poem with which of the following characteristics would be BEST to use to introduce a second-grade class to the genre of poetry?

    A. a haiku about recess

    B. a poem written in free verse about making new friends

    C. a poem that has an easy-to-follow meter and is about going to school

    D. one stanza excerpted from a long poem about being young

Text Types by Author's Purpose

Text can also be classified based on the author's purpose for writing. There are four main writing **styles** that students learn in elementary school:

1. **expository writing:** This style of writing is primarily used to explain an idea or concept or to inform the reader about a topic. It is most often used in formal essays that include a main idea and supporting details based on fact.
2. **narrative writing:** This style of writing is primarily used to tell a personal or fictional story that entertains the reader. The author includes descriptive details and figurative language in order to maintain the reader's attention with dynamic characters, interesting settings, and captivating plots. Poems that tell stories, or **narrative poems**, also use this writing style.
3. **descriptive writing:** This style of writing emphasizes the production of imagery using words and figurative language that appeal to the reader's five senses. It is a writing style that produces vivid pictures in the reader's imagination and is often used to write poetry or detailed descriptions of experiences or events.
4. **persuasive writing:** This style of writing is used to convince, or persuade, a reader to subscribe to the author's opinion or point of view. It follows a formal progression that aims to sway the reader into accepting the author's stance and often plays on the reader's emotions in order to achieve its goal. Persuasive writing is often used for **speeches** and **advertisements**.

Practice Question

5) Which of the following can be classified as persuasive writing?

    A. an advertisement for a new product

    B. a research paper on the effects of climate on ecosystems

    C. a poem about the ocean on a foggy day

    D. a short story with a suspenseful plot

Literary Devices

Alliteration is the repetition of the same sound in nearby words ("the *rotund rhinoceros roared*"). Texts may also contain **analogies**, or comparisons to unlike things for the purpose of explanation. For example, a text may have the following sentence:

You might not think a pet snake and a pet cat are similar, but snakes are like cats in their eating habits and desire to be left alone most of the time.

Analogies are similar to similes; the primary difference is that analogies seek to explain while similes are often used to drive interest and description. Analogies are often employed in argumentative writing to make a point, as in the example above.

Allusions are another feature of some texts. Allusions are indirect references to something else. For example, a text may have the following sentence:

The job of caring for her sister's pets was the cross she had to bear.

The "cross" is an indirect reference to the Christian Bible. Many allusions are to religious or mythical texts; others are historical or allusions to other popular literary texts.

Hyperbole, or exaggerated language, allows writers to emphasize certain traits, feelings, or events; however, it is understood that the words used are not to be taken literally. For example, in the following sentence the writer uses hyperbole to emphasize the speaker's intense desire to see a performer; however, it is understood that the speaker would not literally sacrifice a limb to do so:

I'd give my left arm to see one of her concerts.

Personification is a figure of speech that involves giving abstract ideas or inanimate objects qualities that are human. For example, in the following sentence the reader can conclude that the flowers are in desperate need of being watered; however, since flowers cannot actually *beg*, this an example of personification:

The wilted flowers begged for water.

Onomatopoeia is the use of words that phonetically sound like what they are describing. Words such as *buzz*, *eek*, and *meow* are common examples of onomatopoeia.

> **Check Your Understanding:**
>
> What is the difference between analogy, simile, and metaphor?

Practice Question

Structural Elements of Literature

The structural elements of literature, such as characters, setting, conflict, plot, resolution, point of view, and theme can be introduced alongside other literacy activities, even with students who are pre-readers. The following elements can be included in guided reading while asking the following types of questions:

- "Who are the characters on this page?" (characters)

- "Where does this story happen?" (setting)

- "Why was _____mad/happy/worried, etc?" (conflict/plot)

- "What happened after_____?"

- "How was (the problem) fixed?" (conflict/plot/resolution)

Although **point of view**, or the perspective from which the story is told (first person, *I*, *we*; third person, *he*, *she*, *it*, or *they*; sometimes second person, *you*), may be harder for very young students to grasp, teachers can begin introducing the basic concept of differing points of view by reading the **narrator's** part in one voice and each different character in a different voice and encouraging students to do the same. For older students, second-person point of view can be practiced by reading and writing letters to other students, the teacher, administrators, or other school personnel.

The Authority in Teacher Certification

Practice Question

7) Of the following options, what is the BEST way in which a teacher could introduce a first-grade class to the concept of point of view?

    A. reading a new book that features only one character

    B. asking students to make up voices for each character in a book they already know and use those voices when reading

    C. reading a new book to students and having the teacher change his voice with each new character

    D. asking students to bring a favorite book from home, point out the characters, and explain what each character is thinking

Nonfiction Components and Instructional Strategies

Author's Purpose

Nonfiction texts are written to persuade, inform, explain, entertain, or describe. Authors who write to **persuade** try to convince the reader to act or think a certain way. They may use specific reasons and supporting evidence to do this. Persuasive writers also use **rhetoric**, language chosen specifically for its particular effect, to influence readers.

Writing to **inform** is as straightforward as the term suggests: the author sets out simply to communicate information to the reader. Purely informative writing is found in many textbooks and news articles. Some informational writing may also **instruct** the reader. This type of writing includes items such as lists, steps to be followed, and sequential orders of events.

Similar to informing, some writing **explains**. It might explain how things are similar or different; it might define a term; it might explain a problem and its solution.

Nonfiction may also entertain. Typically, this type of writing will **narrate**, or tell a (true) story. Like fiction, narrative nonfiction (sometimes referred to as literary nonfiction) will include a setting, characters, and a plot. The writer may also use figurative language and other devices to entertain the reader.

Finally, nonfiction texts may **describe** something, such as a detailed description of an event, person, place, or inanimate object.

The acronym **PIEED** helps students think about the author's purpose. It is accompanied by a picture of a pie with various slices to illustrate each of these purposes:

- **p**ersuade
- **i**nform
- **e**xplain
- **e**ntertain

1. Foundations of Language

101

▪   **d**escribe

Author's Purpose

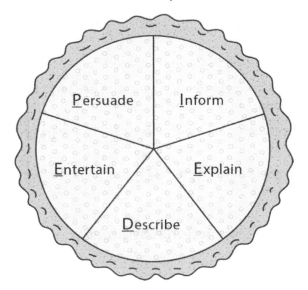

Figure 6.2. PIEED (Author's Purpose)

Nonfiction takes many forms, which are often related to the author's purpose:

- An essay is a short work about a particular topic or idea.
- A speech is a short work with a specific purpose and is intended to be presented orally in front of an audience.
- A news article is a short recounting of a particular story.
- A biography is a detailed, creative textual representation of a person's life.
- An autobiography is an account of an individual's life, told by the individual.

The author's purpose is sometimes further revealed by the text structure:

- A problem-solution text structure is most likely to be used in a persuasive text.
- A compare-and-contrast structure is used to describe two like or unlike things.
- Transitional expressions that are part of the organizational pattern of the text can be used as clues for overall comprehension and in determining the author's purpose.
  - Phrases like "most importantly" and "in contrast" are hints to the author's goal in writing.

Many educators use the following step-by-step process to identify the purpose of a text:

1. While reading the text, think of the question "Why did the author write this?"

2. After reading, complete the statement "The author wrote this mainly to _____." (This is known as the purpose statement.)

3. Find important details in the text that support the purpose statement. If no such details exist, the purpose statement might need to be modified.

Practice Question

8) An teacher is working with fourth-grade students to identify the purpose of a science article in preparation for similar questions on a state assessment. What advice should he give students to help them answer the question "What is the author's purpose?"?

A. to always ask whether the author achieved their purpose for writing the text

B. to look for specific text evidence that supports an assertion about the author's purpose

C. that the purpose will generally be revealed explicitly in the introductory paragraph

D. that a "call to action" never gives possible clues to the author's purpose

Text Structures

Authors organize nonfiction texts with a text structure that suits their purpose. This structure may be a **sequence** of events, such as a news story about the days leading up to an important event. It might also be a thorough **description** of something, as in the opening paragraph of an essay describing a person or place in detail.

Many historical texts use a **cause-and-effect** pattern in which the cause is presented first, and the result is discussed next. A chapter in a social studies text about the Industrial Revolution, for example, might follow this pattern, citing the Industrial Revolution as the cause for a change in working and living conditions in many cities.

Other works are organized in a **problem-solution** structure, in which a problem is presented and then a possible solution discussed. Teachers might introduce this structure through a collaborative activity in which students identify a problem in the classroom, school, or community. They can then write a letter to a decision-maker about the issue and a possible solution. Finally, students can read other problem-solution texts to see how other authors structure their arguments.

Students can use a **compare-and-contrast** structure to explain how two things from their everyday experiences are similar and different. Charts and other graphic organizers can help students organize their thoughts and understand this structure. A teacher might ask students, for example, to use a **Venn diagram** to determine the similarities and differences presented in a text.

It is helpful to integrate reading and writing nonfiction/expository texts that use the same text structure. This approach is used in many textbooks as well as curricular resources based on the Common Core State Standards Initiative.

Practice Question

9) An eighth-grade teacher is working with an interdepartmental team to plan a cross-curricular lesson on world history and English. One of the objectives is based on the following Literacy in History/Social Studies standard:

Compare the point of view of two or more authors for how they treat the same or similar topics, including which details they include and emphasize in their respective accounts (CCSS.ELA-Literacy. RH 9-10.6).

Which activity is MOST appropriate?

- A. Students watch two recorded lectures by famous historians with two different perspectives on the fall of the Roman Empire.
- B. Students read Shakespeare's *Julius Caesar* and then compare it to the information about Caesar in their history text.
- C. Students read Shakespeare's *Richard III* and compare and contrast it with *Julius Caesar*.
- D. Students watch a film about some aspect of Roman history and compare it with the information in their history text.

Key Ideas and Details

Proficient reading requires an ability to use key ideas and details from literary or informational texts to determine the moral, theme, or central idea; make inferences; and summarize information. Readers must also be able to analyze characters, setting, plot, and relationships among ideas, events, and concepts.

The **theme** of a literary text is the basic idea that the author wants to convey. It weaves in and out of the text as the story, play, or poem unfolds. It expresses an underlying opinion related to the text's subject.

On the other hand, the **moral** of a literary text is the lesson the author wants to teach the reader. It is more direct than a theme. The basic underlying idea of informational texts is referred to as the **central idea**. This is the major focus of the information provided in the text.

> ### Check for Understanding:
>
> Consider the familiar story of "The Tortoise and the Hare." What is the central idea of the story? What is the theme of the story? How do they differ?

The goal of teaching reading comprehension is not just to have students arrive at conclusions, but to come to *evidence-based* conclusions. Accordingly, students are urged to formulate responses to and interpretations of the texts they read; then, they must cite specific **details** or **evidence** to support their conclusions.

In the early grades, students begin by referring to the text when looking for answers to teacher-provided questions. When they get older, they move to asking their own questions and quoting text to articulate their answers. By middle school, they should be able to cite details in the text in order to explain and justify their thinking.

In addition to using evidence themselves, students must also be able to identify and interpret an author's use of evidence in the context of an informational text. They must learn how to evaluate arguments based on the evidence and claims made in support of those arguments. One of the most efficient ways of having

students evaluate the reliability of an article is to have them explore how well the writer supported her ideas. An effective teacher might have students first identify the claims of an article, and then look for the evidence the writer includes to substantiate the claim. Evidence can then be evaluated based on its source.

Students should be aware that, even in informational texts, they will have to draw their own **inferences** to fully make sense of what they are reading. Readers draw **inferences** when they use their own knowledge in combination with details from the text to understand the meaning of a sentence, paragraph, or passage.

Summarization is the distillation and condensation of a text into its main idea and key details. It is a short encapsulation of what the text is about and clarifies the general message. To properly summarize fictional texts, it is important to identify **story elements** in a text, which include the following:

- **characters** (e.g., main, minor, protagonist, antagonist, dynamic, static)
- **setting** (where the story takes place)
- **plot** development (e.g., exposition, rising action, problem/climax, falling action, resolution)

Understanding the role of a character in a story via the character's actions, traits, relationships, and personality is **character analysis**. Analyzing how a character thinks and behaves allows a reader to understand the character's motivations and beliefs.

Charts and graphic organizers are tools that support students as they draw meaning from content. **Graphic organizers** provide ways of organizing ideas and information in order to clarify thinking. The following are just some of the main types of reading comprehension graphic organizers:

- **KWL chart:** This is a three-column chart with the headings *K*, *W*, and *L*. The first column lists what students already *know* (K) about a topic; the second column lists what students *want* (W) to know about a topic; and the third column lists what students *learned* (L) from reading about the topic.

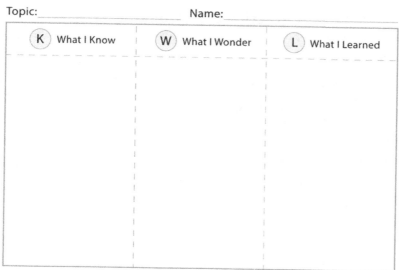

Figure 6.3. KWL Chart

- **Venn diagram:** This is a diagram that is used to compare and contrast texts that treat similar stories or topics in different ways. For example, a teacher may read the same fairy tale told by two

different authors. Students could then use Venn diagrams to organize the similarities and differences between the two stories.

- **sequencing chart:** This organizer is used by students to correctly order the events in a story or the steps in a procedure. Students either arrange picture cards or sentences, or draw pictures and write sentences.
- **main idea/key detail chart:** This chart is an organizational aid for recording the main idea of an informational text and the key details that support the main idea. Prior to using the organizer, students learn how to search introductory and concluding paragraphs for main ideas and body paragraphs for supporting details.
- **fact and opinion chart:** This organizer provides columns where students construct lists of facts and opinions encountered in text. Students learn that facts are truths proven with hard evidence, while opinions are thoughts or beliefs that are unproven. Students learn to look for numerical clues to determine facts and word clues such as *believe* and *should* to determine opinions. In later grades, student use their knowledge of facts and opinions to identify **reasoned judgments**, or points of view supported by reasons and evidence.
- **problem and solution diagram:** This diagram is an organizational aid for recording the central problem in a story and the events that lead to its resolution.
- **plot pyramid:** This visual is an organizational aid for identifying the plot development in a story. With an understanding of the characteristics of exposition, rising action, climax, falling action, and resolution, students can delve deeper into an author's reasons for using particular events, dialogue, and literary devices to move a story forward.
- **text structure chart:** This is a tool that prompts students to identify the relationships between ideas in a text and the signal words that reveal those relationships. Signal words provide clues to the structure an author is using to present information. For example, a sequencing text structure will include signal words such as *first*, *next*, and *last*. A cause-and-effect structure will include signal words and terms such as *consequently*, *as a result*, and *in order to*.

Practice Questions

10) What is an inference based on?

A. facts and specific examples in the text

B. textual details and the reader's own knowledge

C. understanding the author's purpose

D. recognizing the author's tone

11) A teacher notices that a group of students who have just finished reading the same novel are having difficulty identifying how the story transitions from one stage to another. Which of the following is the BEST graphic organizer to help students understand the story's development?

  A. a plot pyramid

  B. a Venn diagram

  C. a main idea/key details chart

  D. a sequencing chart

Identifying Central Ideas

A nonfiction text contains a central or main idea. Identifying this idea is an important—though sometimes challenging—skill for students. This step is part of a process in which students master simpler skills before moving on to more advanced ones:

1. Students practice identifying the **topic** of the text. For example, the topic of a text might be "horses."
2. Students ask themselves a question such as "What is the author saying about horses?"
3. The answer to that question is the central idea of the text. "Horses are animals that have helped humans throughout history."

When using this method, students should not confuse topic with main idea. They should use the identification of the topic to determine the main or central idea.

The main idea of the text is stated explicitly or implicitly. When stated explicitly, the main idea is referred to as a **thesis** or thesis statement. Students can practice identifying the thesis of a short text before studying text with an implicitly stated main idea.

An implicit main idea is more difficult to identify. Students must **synthesize**, or put together, information and details from many parts of the text. The following process can help students identify the main idea:

1. Identify the main idea of each paragraph first. It might be stated explicitly as a topic sentence, or it might be implicit. If the idea is implicit, students will need to summarize the paragraph in a single sentence in their own words.
2. After determining the main idea of each paragraph, students can think about what these main ideas have in common or make a "summary of summaries."
3. Students should check their main idea statements to make sure they have no specific details or examples and that they encapsulate only the most important points.

Because identification of the central idea and summarization are similar thought processes, these skills are often taught together. Teachers might also introduce the central idea as the most important idea within the summary.

Students can use text organization and text features, like headings and bolded terms, to help them distinguish between central ideas and supporting details. Finally, students should understand that identifying the main idea of the text overall (and often of each paragraph) is not a skill to be used in isolation; rather, it is a critical part of actively reading any nonfiction text.

Practice Question

12) A reading interventionist is working with a small group of third-grade students to identify the main idea. When asked, "What is the main idea of the article?" students say, "Jupiter." What question should the interventionist ask NEXT to guide students to identify the main idea?

    A. "What did you already know about Jupiter before reading?"

    B. "What are some new things you learned about Jupiter after reading?"

    C. "What is the author trying to teach us about Jupiter?"

    D. "What did you think was most interesting about Jupiter?"

Nonfiction Texts Across the Curriculum

Students encounter nonfiction texts throughout their coursework. Teachers are therefore tasked with selecting and using nonfiction texts across the various content areas. Doing this might include any or all of the following recommendations:

- **Leveled nonfiction texts** can be used in multiple settings.
    - Content area teachers can use texts on the same topic divided by complexity.
    - Sites like the Smithsonian's *TweenTribune* and *Newsela* offer a variety of science and social studies texts for readers of all levels.
- Persuasive or argumentative texts that cover both sides of an issue can be used across the content areas to spark discussion and encourage analysis at a higher level.
    - When using such texts for instruction, teachers should ask students to analyze the author's rhetoric and use of hyperbole.
    - Students should also determine whether a piece of persuasive writing has used any **logical fallacies**—errors in reasoning that weaken the argument.
- Nonfiction texts that are highly descriptive or that seek to describe a real-life work of art in words can be used as a springboard for creative expression in an art, music, or theater class.
- Students should be given explicit instruction in reading their textbooks or other resources in each course.
    - For example, a science teacher might say, "As you read, underline or highlight the main idea in each paragraph and circle any words you do not know."
    - This type of direction encourages active reading and makes reading assignments more meaningful.
- Nonfiction texts should be carefully selected based on readability and appropriateness as well as alignment to standards.
    - Teachers might be asked to review resources and make curricular recommendations for resources across content areas.

Practice Question

13) A teacher is trying to meet the needs of English language learners in a unit on parts of a plant, since the textbook chapter is not wholly accessible to some students. What should the teacher recommend?

A. to use graphic aids, like diagrams and images, in the text as much as possible in order to promote understanding

B. to assign each student a peer tutor to read the textbook chapter aloud in order to ensure correct pronunciation

C. to provide English language learners with an audio recording of the textbook chapter to listen to multiple times

D. to avoid using the textbook chapter and focus instruction on lectures and note-taking to meet the needs of all learners

Nonfiction Instructional Strategies

Comprehension strategies for nonfiction texts are similar to those for fiction texts, though nonfiction texts might be less predictable in purpose and structure. In expository texts, the writer wants to teach, or *expose*, something to the reader. That means that students are learning something new from a factual perspective while also analyzing rhetorical techniques. Many of the strategies previously mentioned for literary texts can also be used for nonfiction texts, but there are additional considerations.

Students will encounter nonfiction texts more often than fiction texts both across the curriculum and in their everyday lives. They should therefore be given plenty of strategies for overall comprehension of nonfiction texts. By helping students draw connections between what they already know, teachers can aid students into tapping into or activating their background knowledge. The following strategies can help accomplish this:

- With a **brainstorm web**, teachers write the subject of the text in the center and encourage students to fill in the rest of the web with information they already know about the topic.
- An **ABC brainstorm** can be done in either small groups or as a class. With this strategy, students write one word or phrase they already know about the topic for each letter of the alphabet.
- A **free brainstorm** involves asking students to freely write down (or draw) what they already know about a topic.

Students might be unfamiliar with certain terms they need to know in order to fully understand a nonfiction text. Teachers can help students by introducing subject-specific or challenging vocabulary before and during the reading. Strategies to introduce vocabulary include the following:

- **Word Expert:** This strategy involves breaking up new vocabulary words into mini lists and having each student become the "expert" of two or three words by letting them create a card with a definition, illustration, and sentence from the text to share with the class.

- **Words Alive:** With this strategy, students form groups to come up with actions or poses that illustrate the meaning of each new word on their list after the teacher explains the words' meanings to the group.
- **semantic mapping:** Students write the new word in the center and then around it write a synonym, an antonym, an example, and a non-example of the word.
  - ○ Another take on this is the Frayer Model, in which students write the word in the middle of four squares: definition, characteristics, examples, and non-examples.

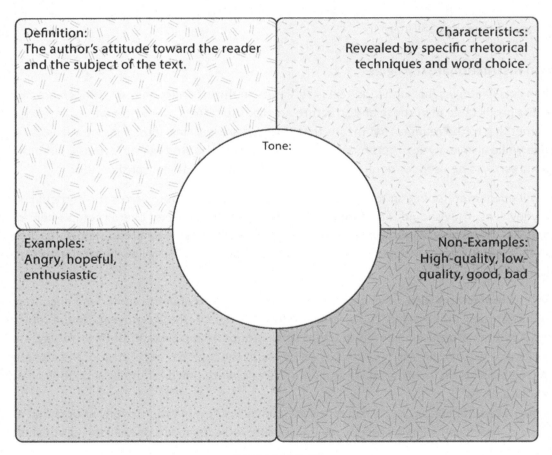

Figure 6.4. Frayer Model

Collaborative learning strategies can be used to tackle challenging nonfiction texts. Students can be divided into pairs for reading activities. They can also be placed in larger groups where each member works on a different part of the text (e.g., one student identifies the main idea of each paragraph and one student identifies the purpose).

Students should be taught and encouraged to use various annotation strategies. They should be encouraged to mark up the text, write in the margins, or use sticky notes. Using **text coding** can help students develop metacognition skills:

- = (information I already know/reminds me of)
- X (not what I expected)
- (important)
- ? (question about this)
- ?? (really confused by this)
- ! (surprising)
- L (learned something new)
- RR (reread section)

In addition to annotating, students can use the following systematic **note-taking strategies:**

- completing a full or partial outline of the text from a template
- using two-column notes to put main ideas on one side and important details on the other (i.e., the **split-page method** or the **two-column method**)
- using the **Cornell method** (Figure 6.5.) whereby each page is divided into keywords, notes, and summaries

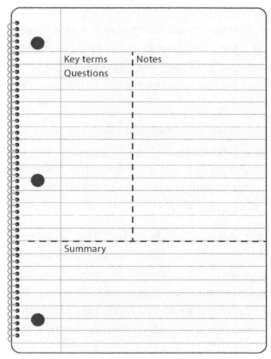

Figure 6.5. Cornell Method for Taking Notes

Finally, students should be given a toolbox of fix-up strategies for when comprehension breaks down. These might be similar to the following strategies used for fiction texts:

- Students should know when and how to use the glossary in each textbook.
- Students should have access to an age- and skill level-appropriate dictionary to consult as needed.
- Students should know whom to go to and how to ask for assistance when they have exhausted all of their independent strategies.

Practice Question

14) Which of the following is the BEST nonfiction comprehension strategy for first-grade students?

A. the Cornell method

B. Words Alive

C. the two-column method

D. text coding

Integration and Application of Knowledge

Once a student can decode a text and determine its meaning, the student must then be able to apply that knowledge. Students should be able to evaluate the argument presented by the author in a text. This includes identifying the author's reasoning and the evidence supporting it, and then determining the sufficiency, relevance, and quality of that reasoning.

For students to do this effectively, teachers must guide them in assessing sources. Students must also understand basic logical reasoning. Teachers should ask students to explain the relationships between evidence and argument. For example, when reading an informational text, teachers can ask students to identify the main idea of a particular section and then point to details in the section that support that main idea.

Teachers should also provide students the opportunity to practice developing their own arguments and reasoning supported by source-based evidence. In the early grades, this involves simple writing assignments, primarily based on personal opinion and experience. As students develop, they should be able to address a broader range of topics and draw on a variety of high-quality academic sources. Similarly, by middle school, students should be able to critique a wide variety of academic writing.

In addition to evaluating evidence, students must learn how to integrate information across multiple texts. This integration can take several different forms. Information from multiple sources can be synthesized to create a fuller understanding of a concept. As discussed in "Identifying Central Ideas," synthesis involves taking specific details about a topic from multiple sources and layering them. For example, a student researching frogs might read an encyclopedia entry, a *National Geographic* article, and a poem. Each source provides different information that the student then brings together to create a unified understanding of frogs.

Secondly, information from different sources can also be *compared* to determine similarities and differences in the approaches, styles, and ideas of different authors. To do this effectively, students must be able to identify both the purposes and biases of the authors.

Finally, students should be able to *analyze* the format of different sources to understand how different forms lead to different tones and meanings in a text. This includes evaluating the role that illustrations and visual representations play in the reader's understanding of a text. For example, in an early-grade classroom, the teacher might read a book aloud to the class in which the visuals provide information beyond the text of the book. The teacher would then encourage students to discuss what the images convey and how that information relates to the text.

Application of knowledge from a text also involves extrapolating information from one source and applying it to new sources, new contexts, and new ideas. As students develop, they should be able to use existing knowledge to make sense of new texts, and then apply the knowledge learned to other new ideas or problems. The teacher can aid students in developing this skill by using the charts and graphic organizers discussed earlier. The curriculum should also include a repetition of knowledge and skills in different contexts to aid students in making connections among concepts.

Practice Questions

15) A student is studying mammals. After learning about characteristics of whales, the student hypothesizes about the characteristics of hippos. What is the student demonstrating?

  A. The student is synthesizing information.

  B. The student is applying knowledge to a new context.

  C. The student is comparing ideas and concepts.

  D. The student is analyzing the format of a text.

16) Which of the following activities would BEST help students evaluate an author's argument?

  A. drawing a Venn diagram

  B. create a diagram of the claim and evidence

  C. examining a second source at a lower reading level

  D. writing a short essay summarizing the argument

Selecting Texts

Selecting Appropriate Texts

Most children's earliest experiences with reading are with **picture books**. Timeless titles such as *Have You Seen My Duckling?* and *Pancakes for Breakfast* can be appreciated by young children and their parents alike, and being read to from a young age is positively associated with future interest in reading. Picture books help young children engage in "pretend reading" by recounting a story from memory or using a picture book to "read" to a sibling or parent.

It is important that educators avoid relegating picture books to the discard pile too early or chide children for their enjoyment of **graphic novels**. Graphics have a place in enhancing interest and the comprehension of texts and are prevalent in much of the written media that is consumed in daily life. In fact, **visual**

Did You Know?

Reading to children has a strong correlation to future achievement. According to the Programme for International Student Assessment (PISA), results from fourteen countries indicate that students whose parents read books to them during the first year of school average fourteen points higher on a reading assessment taken at age fifteen.

literacy—the ability to comprehend visual texts—is an important predecessor to being able to comprehend more sophisticated written works.

Finding a balance between the complexity of a text and an individual student's current level of literacy development can be challenging. Many programs recognize this challenge and structure goal setting and student assessments using a growth-over-time approach. Regardless of the milestones laid out by a school or district, teachers should always aim for students to tackle ever more sophisticated texts as they develop the foundational skills they need to take on new challenges; however, this does not mean that students should be pushed beyond what they can decode. Giving students developmentally inappropriate texts may lead to a denigration of confidence and a lack of interest and enthusiasm for reading.

Many factors contribute to a text's complexity. Before determining appropriateness, texts should be evaluated qualitatively, quantitatively, and per their match to the reader. Quantitative measurements include anything for which a number can be calculated, such as **word frequency**, length of words and **sentence length**, average syllables per word, and so on. These quantitative calculations may result in a range or score being given to a text. The most popular of these are those calculated by **MetaMetrics**, a company that uses word frequency and sentence length in an equation that yields a score. MetaMetrics assigns scores to both readers and texts. Scores assigned to readers typically come from standardized tests and measure a student's current level of reading ability; these are called **reader measures**.

MetaMetrics also assigns **Lexile measures** to texts. While these ranges do not have a direct correlation to grade level in the strictest sense, charts can be used to glean the typical ranges for a given grade. The company purports that the best results come when the reader measure falls within a "sweet spot" range per the text measure.

More than likely, much of what students read (textbooks, passages in software programs, published children's literature) has already been assigned a Lexile text measure. Teachers can raise students' chances of enjoyment and comprehension of texts by ensuring that the Lexile measure fits within the average range for the grade level and, more importantly, for the individual student's reader measure (see Table 6.1.).

Did You Know?

MetaMetrics also offers Lexile measures for Spanish-language texts.

Table 6.1. Lexile Reader and Text Measures for Grades 1 – 12

Grade	Reader Measures, Midyear *25th to 75th Percentile* This is the typical range of reading ability for students in each grade. These measures are designed to help compare a student's level to a typical range; they are not intended to be standards.	Text Measures These text measures have been revised from previous measures to better align with the Common Core State Standards for English Language Arts to ensure that students will meet these standards and be "college and career ready" by the end of high school.
1	BR120L to 295L	190L to 530L
2	170L to 545L	420L to 650L
3	415L to 760L	520L to 820L
4	635L to 950L	740L to 940L
5	770L to 1080L	830L to 1010L
6	855L to 1165L	925L to 1070L
7	925L to 1235L	970L to 1120L
8	985L to 1295L	1010L to 1185L
9	1040L to 1350L	1050L to 1260L
10	1085L to 1400L	1080L to 1335L
11 and 12	1130L to 1440L	1185L to 1385L

> **Helpful Hint:**
>
> Lexile measures are only effective for texts that follow a typical structure. They are not effective for poetry and drama—these types of texts must be measured for complexity using other methods.

There are, of course, other metrics for measuring the readability of a text. Scales such as the Flesch-Kincaid Grade Level, the Gunning-Fog Index, and the ATOS and SMOG indexes may also provide text analytics. A specific program or school may also use other proprietary tools, such as Accelerated Reader Book Finder or Scholastic Book Levels.

Beyond the quantitative measures determined by Lexile and others are qualitative measures, such as the layout of the text (illustrations, text size); the overall text **structure** (simple narrative chronology, more advanced argumentative essay); **sentence structure** (prevalence of simple or more complex sentences); **levels of meaning** (whether ideas are explicitly or implicitly communicated); and **knowledge demand** (the cultural knowledge or other ideas that the reader must already know). The overall language and **vocabulary** of the text also generally fall under qualitative measures, although some quantitative scales measure the frequency of vocabulary with which students of a particular age or grade are unlikely to be familiar.

No single measure of any text can determine appropriateness for all students. For example, Lexile ranges do not account for mature subject matter. Teachers also need to differentiate literacy instruction in the classroom. While literacy development requires reading more and more complex texts, students do not benefit from inaccessible reading material. In fact, this can lead to bad habits such as guessing at or

skipping unfamiliar words instead of trying to decode and asking for help before figuring out an unfamiliar word or text.

Whichever strategy a program uses to address the individualization of reading instruction (e.g., pull-out, push-in, small groups, teacher intervention), teachers must find a just-right level of text complexity where students are challenged but not frustrated. Text complexity is highly individualized and should be matched to the instructional task:

- Texts at the **independent reading level** (for independent reading) require students to read with 99 percent accuracy and 90 percent comprehension. These are generally texts just "below" a student's reading level.

- **Instructional reading level** texts are used for teacher-guided instruction and are typically read at 85 percent accuracy with over 75 percent comprehension. These texts are usually "at" the student's reading level.

- **Frustration-level** texts are those read at less than 85 percent accuracy and less than 50 percent comprehension. These texts are generally "above" a student's reading level and are not recommended. New research, however, suggests that such texts might be effective in paired reading activities with proficient readers.

In addition to selecting texts based on text measures, educators should consider other factors that depend on age. The following questions are good to ask when selecting appropriate texts for early-childhood classroom instruction:

- Does the text introduce or reinforce concepts introduced in the curriculum (e.g., sight word acquisition, phonemic awareness, letter sounds)?

- Does the text have picture/text correlation that will hold readers' attention and provide comprehension clues?

- Does the text teach an important lesson or moral?

- Are the characters and situations diverse and engaging?

The following questions should guide the selection of texts for students:

- Are texts aligned to instructional goals?

- Are texts at the appropriate level (instructional or independent) for the planned activity?

- Are texts relevant and aligned to student interests?

- Do texts promote deep comprehension or analysis?

- Do texts contain highly specialized or nuanced vocabulary that students may not be familiar with?

- Do texts offer **multimodal elements** (i.e., appealing to different modes of communication, such as written text, spoken language, and visual images) that might be relevant for instructional objectives?

When students are **self-selecting texts**, or choosing something to read based on their own interests, they may still need scaffolding from educators. Knowing a student's personality, interests, and independent reading level can be helpful in this regard; however, even independent reading levels can evolve. Some

students may seek out and enjoy more challenging texts, while others may become frustrated at that level. Knowledge of the individual student should guide suggestions.

Practice Questions

17) What is one disadvantage of relying on Lexile level as the sole indicator of text appropriateness?

   A. It is only applicable to students whose first language is English.

   B. It fails to account for qualitative text features.

   C. It does not encourage the reading of rigorous texts.

   D. It can only be used to measure fiction texts.

18) What is the BEST way to differentiate instruction in a first-grade reading classroom?

   A. practice oral reading with only the more advanced students so that those struggling will not feel uncomfortable

   B. use only texts on the lower end of the first-grade Lexile range to ensure that they are accessible to all students

   C. set aside time for students to engage in silent reading with a teacher-selected book based on student ability and interests

   D. conduct additional phonics drills with students who need help with decoding while the other students do a science experiment

Answer Key

1) C: The *Frog and Toad* series of books (Arnold Lobel) is the only answer option that is not an example of nonfiction; it is a fictitious book series that teaches students about the value of friendship. Autobiographies and biographies are both nonfiction. *TweenTribune* contains news articles curated for younger audiences and is also an example of nonfiction.

2) C: Previewing the booklet's title and illustrations and making predictions about the book will help the student determine the book's genre.

3) B: Drama is particularly useful for reader's theater, in which students read parts of a text aloud and develop oral reading skills and prosody, or expressive reading.

4) C: A poem with an easy-to-follow meter (i.e., beat, rhythm) is the best of these answer options since students can become engaged with the material by being encouraged to clap, dance, stomp, etc. to the beat of the poem.

5) A: Persuasive writing aims to influence the reader to agree with what is stated and to act accordingly. The purpose of an advertisement is to convince the reader to buy a product.

6) B: An audio recording would help students who are challenged by reading written text to understand the concepts of rhyme and meter.

7) C: At the first-grade level, teachers can introduce students to the basic concept of differing points of view by reading the narrator's part in one voice and each different character in a different voice and then encouraging students to do the same once the concept is grasped. Option B might be a good strategy to use once the students have already been introduced to the concept of point of view.

8) B: Supporting text evidence is key to confirming answers on such a test and in confirming the author's purpose.

9) B: Studying Shakespeare's *Julius Caesar* and comparing it to the relevant information in the history text involves two different texts by two different authors. Students can compare things such as purpose (inform versus entertain) and why certain points were or were not emphasized.

10) B: In order to read between the lines, readers must use their own knowledge as well as draw on the information provided.

11) A: A plot pyramid helps students identify and visualize how an author moves a story forward in clear stages, with specific characteristics: exposition, rising action, climax, falling action, and resolution.

12) C: This question can help students narrow a topic to the main idea.

13) A: Graphic text features will help all learners, including English language learners, to understand key concepts visually, even if they lack the vocabulary skills to read the textbook chapter.

14) B: Even first-grade students can "act out" the meaning of new words and would therefore likely find a Words Alive activity engaging.

15) B: Whales and hippos are both mammals, so the student is using the former to understand the latter.

16) B: The strength of an author's argument is in the connection between claim and evidence.

17) B: Lexile measures only account for quantitative text features, such as word length and sentence length. They do not measure content, knowledge demands, and so on.

18) C: This activity would allow for the differentiation of text complexity.

7. Meeting the Needs of Students

Students with Reading Difficulties and Disabilities

Legal Issues Related to Reading Disabilities

Today's special education landscape has been shaped by federal legislation over the last fifty years. Before federal legislation mandated school access, many individuals with disabilities were institutionalized rather than given opportunities for education. In institutions, systemic neglect and abuse was common. In the 1960s, alongside other civil rights movements, the disability rights movement raised public awareness of the treatment of individuals with disabilities. The federal government responded with legislation supporting educational opportunities for people with disabilities.

In 1965, Congress enacted the **Elementary and Secondary Education Act (ESEA)**, which seeks to improve student academic achievement through supplementary educational services as well as increased educational research and training. It also provides financial assistance to schools that service a high percentage of students from low-income (Title I funding) families. ESEA was the first legislation to provide states with direct financial assistance to support the education of students with disabilities.

> ### Did You Know?
>
> In 1970, only one in five children with disabilities attended US schools; in fact, many states at that time had laws excluding students with certain disabilities from school.

A major civil rights victory for individuals with disabilities came with the **Rehabilitation Act of 1973**, which ensures all students with disabilities a right to public education. **Section 504** of the Rehabilitation Act prohibits programs that receive federal financial assistance from discriminating on the basis of disability. As federally funded institutions, public schools are required to ensure that students with disabilities receive a comparable education to those without disabilities. If a student with a disability does not qualify for services under IDEA, the student may still receive support through a 504 plan. Under Section 504, students with disabilities may receive related services, accommodations, and modifications to ensure equal access to education.

The most comprehensive civil rights legislation for individuals with disabilities to date is the 1990 **Americans with Disabilities Act (ADA)**. The ADA prohibits discrimination on the basis of disability in the workplace and in all public places (e.g., restaurants, parks, schools, businesses). The passage of the ADA has led to increased community access, accessibility of public transportation, and more equal employment opportunities for individuals with disabilities. As a comprehensive civil rights law, the ADA provides another layer of legal protection for the right of students with disabilities to have equal access to public education.

The first legislation targeting educational rights was the 1975 **Education for All Handicapped Children Act** (EAHCA or EHA, also referred to as **P.L. 94-142**). This act expands educational rights for students with disabilities. The legislation ensures that students with disabilities can access any accommodations, modifications, related services, and specially designed instruction needed to make adequate educational progress in a public school setting.

Congress reauthorized EHA as the **Individuals with Disabilities Education Act (IDEA)** in 1990 and again with amendments in 1997 and 2004. Part B of IDEA provides for services for students between the ages of three and twenty-one, while Part C provides for early intervention services for students from birth to three years old.

Since its original authorization, IDEA has operated under six foundational principles:

- **Free Appropriate Public Education (FAPE):** FAPE maintains that students with disabilities have a right to an education at no additional cost to parents. (Parents of students with disabilities are still responsible for school fees that apply to all students.) The education is required to meet the student's unique educational needs in a public school setting.

- **Appropriate and nondiscriminatory evaluation:** Evaluations must be completed by a team of trained professionals (e.g., teachers, school psychologists) and should include information from parents. Evaluations should address all areas of concern, and materials must be sound and nondiscriminatory. Evaluations must be conducted in a timely manner, and reevaluations must occur a minimum of every three years.

- **Individualized Education Program (IEP):** An IEP is a legal document developed by the IEP team (parents, general educators, special educators, administrators, related service providers) that reports present levels of performance, annual goals and objectives, accommodations, modifications, related services, and specially designed instruction to help students make adequate educational progress.

- **Least Restrictive Environment (LRE):** Students with disabilities must be provided supports with nondisabled peers to the maximum extent appropriate for them to make educational progress. This includes access to the general curriculum, which ensures that students with disabilities have access to the same curriculum as their nondisabled peers. LRE emphasizes placement in the general education classroom with supplemental aides and services as much as possible.

- **Parent (and student) participation:** Parents must have a shared role in all special education decisions, including IEP reviews, evaluation, and placement decisions.

- **Procedural safeguards:** Parents must receive written notice of procedural safeguards, parent and student rights, meetings, and all educational decisions. Parents have access to all student educational records and may take due process measures in the event of a disagreement with the school district.

The most recent authorization of IDEA is the **2004 Individuals with Disabilities Education Improvement Act**. IDEA 2004 expands procedures for identifying students with learning disabilities to include identification through response to intervention. IDEA 2004 also includes several changes to align with the 2001 **No Child Left Behind (NCLB)** legislation. The main purpose of NCLB is to improve the academic performance of all students through increased accountability for results, emphasizing research-based instruction, and ensuring such instruction is delivered by highly qualified teachers (HQTs).

To replace NCLB, Congress passed the **Every Student Succeeds Act (ESSA)** in 2015; it went into effect for the 2017 – 2018 school year. ESSA rolls back many of the federal education requirements, giving power back to the states. Under ESSA, states are required to create accountability plans, track state-set accountability goals, and incorporate accountability systems (e.g., state assessments, English language proficiency, postsecondary readiness, and school safety). ESSA removes the federal HQT requirement of NCLB; however, each state must set expectations for ensuring that HQTs are providing instruction. Moreover, ESSA maintains the state assessment requirements of NCLB and Title I funding for schools.

Practice Question

1) Which of the following would NOT be a service provided to a student under a 504 plan?

    A. occupational therapy

    B. testing accommodations

    C. extra transition time between classes

    D. specially designed instruction

Characteristics of Reading Difficulties and Disabilities

Students progress toward full literacy at different rates. Those who do not meet—or who are at risk of not meeting—grade-level expectations have reading difficulties, which are different from reading disabilities. Students with **reading difficulties** are falling behind grade-level expectations in reading but do not qualify for special education services under the category of a specific learning disability (SLD). **Reading disabilities**, on the other hand, are formally diagnosed learning disabilities. Students with a diagnosed reading disability will typically qualify for special education services and are served through an IEP.

Students who qualify for special education services under another category (such as intellectual disability, speech and language impairment, or developmental disability) may have other disabilities that cause reading difficulties. Their IEPs may list reading-related modifications and accommodations even though they have not been diagnosed with an SLD.

Reading difficulties fall into three categories:

1. **Specific word-reading difficulties (SWDs)** describe when students have trouble reading or decoding individual words. Students with SWDs may also have below-average fluency and comprehension levels because they struggle to decode on the word level. When presented with texts they are able to decode, however, these students may have strong reading comprehension skills.

2. **Specific reading comprehension difficulties (SRCDs)** are experienced by students who can decode on a basic level but lack the vocabulary knowledge or inferencing skills necessary to fully comprehend texts.

3. **Mixed reading difficulties (MRDs)** describe students who have deficits in both decoding and comprehension.

Reading disabilities fall into three categories:

1. **Phonological deficits** occur when students struggle with word recognition due to weak phonological processing. Students with these deficits face a range of challenges, including trouble

with letter-sound correspondence, sounding out words, and spelling. Seventy to 80 percent of students with a reading-related learning disability have phonological deficits. These deficits are usually described by the term *dyslexia*, sometimes called **language-based learning disability (LBLD)**.

2. **Processing speed/orthographic processing deficits** occur when students do not read quickly or accurately. Orthographic coding differs from phonological coding in that it does not rely solely on letter-sound correspondence and knowledge but rather on memory (of letters, groups of letters, or entire words) to decode. This type of deficit is typically milder than a phonological deficit and may be co-occurring or distinct from a phonological deficit. There is some debate as to whether this type of deficit is a subtype of dyslexia or a distinct disability.

3. **Specific comprehension deficits** describe issues with vocabulary, language learning, and abstract reasoning. Comprehension deficits might co-occur with phonological or processing deficits as well as with other conditions, particularly autism spectrum disorder (ASD). This type of deficit is also referred to as **hyperlexia** because word recognition skills are average or even advanced.

Did You Know?

Dyslexia is a very common SLD that is thought to affect at least 15 percent of the global population.

Practice Question

2) Specific comprehension deficits often co-occur in students diagnosed with which of the following?

A. dyspraxia

B. dysgraphia

C. autism spectrum disorder (ASD)

D. emotional behavioral disorder (EBD)

Assessing Reading Difficulties and Disabilities

Universal screening is an assessment process for possible reading difficulties. It usually takes place three times per year. Schools use different assessment measures for screening; the following are the most common:

- **Curriculum-based measurement (CBM)** is an informal assessment in which a student reads aloud a passage from the core reading curriculum. The student reads for about one to five minutes while the teacher records the number of words read correctly. This value of the number of words correct is compared to the target for the month and year based on predefined standards related to grade and age.

- Published measurements include the **Dynamic Indicators of Basic Early Literacy Skills (DIBELS)**, the **Woodcock Reading Mastery Test–Revised (WJ–R)**, and the **Texas Primary Reading Inventory (TPRI)**. These are more formal assessments that generate reports in greater detail than simple CBM reports do.

Any assessment instrument that is used to screen for reading difficulties should meet the following criteria:

- sensitivity: the degree to which an instrument detects at-risk students
- specificity: the degree to which the instrument avoids false positives
- practicality: the brevity and simplicity of the assessment
- consequential validity: the degree to which the assessment refrains from inequity in identification and is shown to lead to effective intervention

Different states, districts, and schools may establish different criteria for labeling students as at-risk for reading difficulties. Some use a threshold measure, for example: "students who score lower than X or who read fewer than X words correct per minute." Others use norm-references, such as national or state averages. Still others develop their own criterion and may label performance as "satisfactory/unsatisfactory" or "high-risk/low-risk."

Students identified as at-risk during universal screening should be provided support using the response to intervention (RTI) framework. The student may be referred for evaluation of eligibility for special education services at any point during this process based on school district policy and the student's situation. These services may enable some students to receive more targeted or appropriate interventions than they would with existing Tier 2 and Tier 3 intervention frameworks.

> **Did You Know?**
>
> Because of the desire to identify all students who might benefit from interventions for reading difficulties or disabilities, some educational researchers believe the rate of "false positive" identification to be as high as 50 percent.

If students are referred for evaluation for special education services, various instruments can be used to determine the presence of reading-related disabilities (including—but not limited to—dyslexia). These instruments test for skills in phonological awareness, decoding, fluency and comprehension, and rapid naming (a skill linked to reading fluency). The following are just some of these assessment measurements:

- Comprehensive Test of Phonological Processing (CTOPP-2)
- Phonological Awareness Test (PAT-2: NU)
- Test of Word Reading Efficiency (TOWRE-2)
- Gray Oral Reading Test (GORT-5)
- Rapid Automatized Naming Test (RAN/RAS)
- relevant subtests of the Woodcock–Johnson III (WJIII) or the Wechsler Individual Achievement Test (WIAT-III)

RTI and referral for special education services are not mutually exclusive. Tier 2 and 3 reading interventions are used for students with reading difficulties whether or not they qualify for special education services. Targeted reading interventions are not meant as a replacement for special education services.

The model for RTI and/or special education interventions differs among schools. Some schools use a sheltered reading intervention class period for all identified students. The class is made up of students with specific learning disabilities, students with other disabilities that impact reading performance, and students who have reading difficulties but do not qualify for special education.

In another school model, students who qualify for special education services might receive services from special education teachers, while students with reading difficulties receive services from reading interventionists.

Not all schools and districts use an RTI framework. In some settings, students may participate in less formal types of interventions such as voluntary before- or after-school tutoring, summer school, or summer reading programs.

In any model, **progress monitoring** should be used to determine the efficacy of interventions. Curriculum-based measurements are the most popular method of progress monitoring. There are many print and digital tools to organize and analyze this information. Additionally, several publishers and education technology companies provide digital platforms for ongoing progress monitoring, usually with a per-student, subscription-based fee.

Based on the progress monitoring data, the educator must determine the best plan of action for each student. This might include collaboration with other professionals, such as special educators, ESOL teachers, school psychologists, educational diagnosticians, and so on. Educators may have different focuses, but they all share the same goal: student progress in reading.

Practice Question

3) Why would asking first-grade students to write the letters of the alphabet as a screening measure for reading difficulties be in effective?

    A. because it lacks practicality

    B. because it relies too heavily on background knowledge

    C. because it lacks sensitivity

    D. because it relies too heavily on quantitative data

Instructing Students with Reading Difficulties and Disabilities

Students with reading difficulties and disabilities that impact reading performance need explicit, systematic, direct instruction. This model of instruction and practice should be reinforced across settings. For example, students still mastering letter-sound correspondence can practice with charts or flashcards at home.

Additionally, instruction must be based on each student's needs as revealed through assessment and data collection. Instruction not targeted in this way may be ineffective and/or may only increase student frustration.

Instructional strategies and intervention techniques for students with reading difficulties and disabilities are generally provided either to increase word identification or decoding on the word level or to increase overall comprehension. Specific strategies and interventions include the following:

- **Scaffolding** refers to the supports used by teachers (or sometimes peers) during classroom activities. Scaffolds should be built into all lessons per the Universal Design for Learning (UDL), which states that all students should be able to learn from the same curriculum.

- **Shaping** refers to providing incremental reinforcers and is also helpful in instructing students with reading difficulties and disabilities. For example, as students progress by memorizing more grade-level high-frequency words, they should receive frequent, positive feedback from educators. This feedback is important for students who struggle with reading since they may not receive consistent positive reinforcers (e.g., high grades, praise from peers) that other students who excel academically typically receive.

- Students with reading difficulties on the word level benefit most from **phonics instruction**, particularly phoneme blending, phoneme segmentation, and phoneme deletion or substitution practice activities. Synthetic (e.g., Elkonin boxes) or analogy-based phonics approaches (e.g., sorting words into categories based on similarities in structures) are popular instructional methodologies for these students.

- Intensive, **scripted synthetic phonics programs**, such as Direct Instruction programs (published under names like *Reading Mastery, Corrective Reading, Horizons,* and *Funnix*), are also empirically based and generally effective; however, there is some controversy surrounding them, as they use principles of behavioral analysis, such as stimulus-response-feedback as the primary means of instruction.

- Students with reading difficulties on the comprehension level benefit most from instruction and interventions that help them develop metacognition to self-assess understanding and apply strategies to integrate information and synthesize it with existing knowledge. Such strategies include semantic mapping or other visual organizers; reciprocal teaching; and the **PQ4R method**, which is an extension of the SQ3R method (see Chapter 6). In the PQ4R method, students preview the reading material, generate questions, and read to answer the questions. After that, they reflect on what they have read, recite or retell from memory what they have read, and then review the material for any missed information.

In addition to the instructional strategies listed above, students with disabilities, such as dyslexia, that impact reading can benefit from certain accommodations. **Accommodations** are changes to materials or instructional methodologies that allow all students to learn the same material as their peers. Material and instructional accommodations are described in Table 7.1.

Table 7.1. Material and Instructional Accommodations

Materials Accommodations

- underlining or highlighting the key words in directions
- chunking assignments or presenting them in smaller increments
- using a glossary or list of key vocabulary terms
- using chapter-by-chapter, page-by-page, or even paragraph-by-paragraph reading guides
- using assistive technology
  - audio recordings or books on tape
  - e-readers or tablets
  - text-to-speech software

Instructional Accommodations

- clarifying directions through oral repetition and providing a written version

Table 7.1. Material and Instructional Accommodations

- implementing daily routines to clarify expectations
- providing visual aids whenever possible
- encouraging the use of mnemonic devices
- providing students a hard copy of notes
- implementing frequent review and reinforcement activities at the end of each lesson
- reviewing previously learned concepts at the beginning of a new lesson
- creating opportunities for additional or extended practice
- using peer learning strategies

At times, students with reading disabilities will also need modifications to what they are expected to learn. **Modifications** will usually be listed on the student's IEP and may include a reduced number of questions or items on assessments, different grading criteria, and so on. Special education teachers may collaborate with reading specialists to develop and monitor accommodations and modifications for students with learning disabilities that impact reading performance.

Practice Question

4) A first-grade teacher has a student with dyslexia who is very frustrated and feeling overwhelmed by a reading assignment. What should the teacher try to do?

A. have the student read an abridged version of the reading assignment

B. encourage the student to read at least fifty words

C. give the student an audio recording of the reading assignment to aid in comprehension

D. read the entire reading assignment aloud in class, asking a different student to read orally each day

English Language Learners

Second-Language Acquisition

Researchers agree that **second-language acquisition** occurs, much like first-language acquisition, through a series of stages. Learners must pass through each of the five stages on their way to proficiency, though the time spent in each stage varies from person to person.

The first stage—**preproduction**—is also known as the **silent period**. Though these learners may have upward of 500 words in their receptive vocabulary, they refrain from speaking; however, they will listen and may copy words down. Learners in this stage can respond to visual cues, such as pictures and gestures, and they can communicate their comprehension. Sometimes students will repeat what they hear in a process called **parroting**. This can help them build their receptive vocabulary, but it should not be mistaken for producing language.

In the **early production** stage, learners achieve 1,000-word receptive and active vocabularies. They can now produce single-word and two- to three-word phrases and can respond to questions and statements as such. Many learners in this stage enjoy musical games or word plays that help them memorize language chunks (groups of related words and phrases) that they can use later.

English language learners (ELLs) have a vocabulary of about 3,000 words by the time they reach the **speech emergence stage** of second-language acquisition. They are able to chunk simple words and phrases into sentences that may or may not be grammatically correct. They respond to models of proper usage better than they do to explicit correction.

At this stage, learners are more likely to have conversations with native English speakers, as they are gaining confidence in their language skills. These students can understand simple readings when reinforced by graphics or pictures and can complete some content work with support.

> ### Did You Know?
>
> **Morpheme acquisition order** is the pattern in which the knowledge of morphemes is gained as people acquire language. Within first-language acquisition, the pattern remains consistently fixed for most learners. For English language learners, the pattern is less constant and varies based on the learner's first language.

By the **intermediate fluency stage**, English language learners have a vocabulary of about 6,000 words. They can speak in more complex sentences and catch and correct many of their errors. They are also willing to ask questions to clarify what they do not understand. Learners at this stage may communicate fairly well, but they have large gaps in their vocabulary and in their grammatical and syntactical understanding of the language. They are often comfortable with group conversations as long as any difficult academic vocabulary is limited.

Second-language learners reach **advanced fluency** when they have achieved cognitive language proficiency in their learned language. They demonstrate near-native ability and use complex, multi-phrase and multi-clause sentences to convey their ideas. Though learners at this stage still have accents and sometimes use idiomatic expressions incorrectly, they are essentially fluent.

As language learners progress through levels of study, they usually develop an interlanguage to aid them in their progression. **Interlanguage** is the learner's current understanding of the language they are learning. It is a rule-based system that develops over time. It tends to blend aspects of the learner's first language with those of the second.

Interlanguage is often characterized by the learner's tendency to overgeneralize speaking and writing rules in the new language. For example, when students learn that most English verbs in the past tense end in –*ed*, they might apply this rule to all verbs. The learner then creates an interlanguage rule by continuing to conjugate irregular verbs incorrectly. Over time, these rules are adjusted and readjusted according to feedback, and the interlanguage evolves as the learner moves toward proficiency.

When language learners stop progressing and the development of their interlanguage stops, their understanding can become fossilized. **Fossilization** is the point in second-language acquisition when a learner's growth freezes, and further linguistic development becomes highly unlikely.

5) Lucia enjoys listening to songs in English. She memorizes the choruses and sings them to herself. She notes words she does not recognize and integrates phrases from the songs into her everyday language practice. When asked about the songs, Lucia responds in single words and short phrases but struggles to compose complete sentences. In which stage of second-language acquisition might Lucia be?

   A. preproduction

   B. early production

   C. speech emergence

   D. intermediate fluency

First-Language Influence on Second Language

Students' native languages will always impact their learning of English. The influences will occur in all parts of language learning, from grammatical understanding to vocabulary acquisition to syntactical awareness. They are bound to transfer their understanding of their first language to their studies of English in order to make sense of what they are learning.

Transfer occurs when a student applies knowledge of a first language to another. Transfer can be both positive and negative. **Positive transfer** occurs when students find similarities between their native languages and English and use those similarities to help them learn.

For example, a Spanish-speaking student may recognize the English verb "to comprehend" because it looks like the Spanish verb *comprender* ("to understand"). Visually similar words like these are **cognates**. Words that look similar but are different in meaning are **false cognates**. The Spanish verb *comprar*, for example, means "to buy," not "to compare." Students who are learning a new language should understand that both cognates and false cognates exist.

Negative transfer, or interference, occurs when students incorrectly apply rules from their native languages to their learning of English. For example, a Spanish-speaking student may place an adjective after a noun (e.g., "the house red") because of the noun-adjective structure in Spanish. In English, however, the adjective comes before the noun (e.g., "the red house").

> **Did You Know?**
>
> **Cognate awareness** is the ability of students to recognize cognates and use them as tools for understanding a second language.

Code-switching is also frequent among language learners. Students mix in words from their first language with the language they are learning. This happens when they have forgotten a term or do not know how to express themselves in the second language. For example, a Spanish-speaking student who is looking for the bathroom and cannot recall a vocabulary word might ask, "Where is the *baño*?" This type of linguistic back-and-forth is very common with bilingual and multilingual individuals.

Finally, students' **accents** will impact their learning and pronunciation of English. Often speakers will substitute the sounds of their first language for ones they think are the same in English. For example, some Spanish speakers may pronounce the /v/ sound like the English *b*.

Additionally, stresses and intonations of words can be carried from first languages. Both of these speech patterns can change the meanings of English words (e.g., the meanings of the words *read* and *read*), leading to an unclear message.

Practice Question

6) Jamie has just moved from Mexico to California, where his mother enrolled him in an ESOL class. A few weeks in, Jamie is still reluctant to speak because he mixes in words from his first language with the English he is learning. Which linguistic behavior is Jamie demonstrating?

    A. code-switching

    B. cognate awareness

    C. difficulty with accent

    D. language interference

Assessment of English Language Learners

Because English language learners need differentiated instruction, they should be identified as soon as possible. Title III of Part A of ESSA requires states to hold English language learners to the same rigorous standards as all students. These students must receive high-quality, early targeted interventions to increase English proficiency and stay on track to meet grade-level objectives.

The first and most common step in identifying ELLs is the **home language survey**. Many states and districts mandate that parents complete this survey upon student enrollment. The survey is short (fewer than ten questions) and available in multiple languages. An example survey is shown in Figure 7.2.

Student Name:		Grade:	Date:
Parent/Guardian Name: _____ Parent/Guardian Signature: _____			

Right to Translation and Interpretation Services	1. In what language(s) would your family prefer to communicate with the school? _____
Eligibility for Language Development Support	2. What language did your child learn first? _____ 3. What language does your child use the most at home? _____ 4. What is the primary language used in the home, regardless of the language spoken by your child? _____ 5. Has your child received English language development support in a previous school? Yes____ No____ Don't Know____
Prior Education	6. In what country was your child born? _____ 7. Has your child ever received formal education outside of the United States? (Kindergarten – 12th grade) ____Yes ____No If yes: Number of months: _____ Language of instruction: _____ 8. When did your child first attend a school in the United States? (Kindergarten – 12th grade) _____ Month Day Year

Figure 7.2. Home Language Survey

The home language survey is not the end of the process. Some parents might fear that their child will be placed in "lower-level" classes, so they may say that English is spoken in home when it is not. In other cases, students who speak a language other than English at home may be fluent in both languages and require no language learning supports at school; however, in many states and districts, all students who use a language other than English at home must receive further assessment to determine the need for English language learning services. Some commercially available assessment instruments include the following:

- Bilingual Syntax Measure (BSM) of listening and speaking
- IDEA Proficiency Test (IPT)
- Language Assessment System (LAS Links)

- WIDA-ACCESS Placement Test
- Woodcock-Muñoz Language Survey–Revised (WMLS–R)
- Student Oral Language Observation Matrix (SOLOM), which is particularly useful if the second language is not Spanish

Some states also use scores below a certain threshold on standardized achievement tests as possible indications of limited English proficiency, particularly for older students (grades 2 and above).

State requirements for qualifications to administer ELL assessments vary. In some locations, ESOL or bilingual education teachers might give such assessments. In others, reading specialists are responsible, particularly if they are proficient in the student's first language. Reading specialists work closely with teachers and administrators who are specially trained in second language acquisition to make sure the assessment process is thorough and expedient.

If a reading specialist conducting an assessment determines that the student needs to be tested for English proficiency, there should be consultations with the appropriate specialist to ensure that the student is assessed by the most qualified individual.

The assessment is typically followed by an interview with the student's parents or guardians, with an interpreter as needed. This step is crucial since it can give relevant background on the student's prior educational experiences and other factors that might not be apparent through the home language survey and assessment.

In some states, particularly those with many English language learners, a **Language Proficiency Assessment Committee** (LPAC) may be formed. An LPAC, which focuses on language-learning goals, is composed of relevant educators and administrators. This committee recommends placements of ELLs into certain courses and creates plans for their success.

Educators must consider all aspects of a student's learning situation. Formal assessment measures, like standardized tests and other high-stakes assessments, may not fully reflect an ELL's abilities. Educators should use frequent, ongoing informal assessment measures to help confirm any placement decisions made through standardized assessments.

Students who require special education services or reading intervention services are in another category. Many schools and districts use a multidisciplinary approach to identify students for special services. This approach requires input from special education teachers, ESOL teachers, reading specialists, school psychologists, and others.

Students who are misplaced (e.g., those who are thought to have second language acquisition issues when they actually have a learning difference) will not receive appropriate services and programming.

Furthermore, it is not unusual that a student might need English language learning support *and* qualify for special education services. ESOL teachers may initiate referrals for special education services as appropriate. A student might need evaluation by multiple professionals before the best services to meet individual needs are found

Practice Question

7) Which of the following is the MOST appropriate question to ask parents or guardians during an interview as part of a comprehensive assessment of English language learning?

    A. "Do you value education in your home?"

    B. "Has your child attended school before?"

    C. "Why did you come to the United States?"

    D. "Why do you believe learning English is important?"

Instruction of English Language Learners

Like all learners, ELLs need developmentally appropriate systematic instruction to build content knowledge and English proficiency. While students are working to master content-specific standards, they will also be working to master **English Language Proficiency (ELP) standards**. Such standards may be created by the state or by the WIDA Consortium (a group of state and government agencies that uses a shared set of ELPs). These standards aim to help students develop language proficiencies related to language arts, mathematics, science, social studies, and the social and instructional language of the school environment.

<table>
<tr><td>

Did You Know?

Some schools use bilingual education to transition to solely English instruction. Other schools use full English immersion with ESOL services through co-teaching, pull-out services, or sheltered or specialized classes.

</td></tr>
</table>

Within a broader framework of overarching ELPs, educators should create language objectives for ELLs that correspond with each lesson's focus. In schools with a large population of English language learners, some classes may be sheltered. **Sheltered** classes focus on the content area and English language learning, with an emphasis on developing language objectives in conjunction with content area proficiency.

However, if ELL students are taught in the general education setting, content area teachers will need to embed English learning objectives in their lessons. They will also need to modify lessons and assessments in order to meet the needs of all learners. This might include employing the following strategies:

- using picture dictionaries or electronic translators
- eliminating portions of assignments or assessments students may not have background knowledge of
- using peer tutors or collaborative learning strategies that build on each student's strengths
- using multimedia or visual elements to aid in understanding
- pre-teaching core vocabulary or using vocabulary scaffolding, such as digital texts with click-through definitions
- limiting teacher talk and, when used, avoiding colloquialisms and speaking slowly
- verifying that instructions are understood before students begin a task
- providing both print and oral versions of instructions
- using manipulatives or authentic learning situations whenever possible
- providing copies of lecture notes or allowing audio recording

When conducting assessments with English language learners, some common strategies include the following:

- giving students a word bank or other explicit prompting
- allowing a test to be read aloud or to be completed orally in its entirety
- giving written assessments with simplified language
- administering assessments in smaller portions
- allowing students to use a dictionary or translating device on tests and/or allowing for extra time or unlimited time
- not penalizing for spelling or grammar errors (as appropriate)
- using informal assessment measures, such as observational records or oral assessments, whenever possible

Reading and English language arts teachers are in a slightly different position from content area teachers. They must teach basic literacy skills along with the foundations of English as a language with which students might not be familiar. Their focus will be on the following best practices in reading instruction, with an emphasis on the needs of English language learners:

- **phonemic awareness:** English phonemes are distinct and should be taught explicitly, particularly for sounds that do not exist in a student's native language. Sounds that are present in a student's native language and already known by the student can be transferred rapidly. In such cases, instruction in phonemes should focus on those that differ from the students' first language.

- **systematic phonics instruction:** As with all learners, systematic phonics instruction is effective with students whose first language is not English. Decoding through phonics is a two-step process: teachers must give ELLs the tools to sound out words, but these students must also be able to make meaning of the words based on their oral language vocabulary, which should be developed in tandem.

- **automatic word recognition (sight reading):** This strategy can be very helpful for ELLs, can speed up reading rates, and can sometimes prevent difficulties encountered when words deviate from standard phonetic structures.

- **fluency:** Reading fluency follows oral language fluency; however, ELLs may have trouble with strategies that involve reading aloud in front of others. These students may lack confidence and focus on mistakes instead of growth over time. Oral reading practice with English language learners should be carefully orchestrated and make use of a trusted peer whenever possible.

- **vocabulary:** Vocabulary instruction for ELLs will vary considerably from their native-speaking classmates. ELLs will need instruction in idioms and basic "connector words" like *because, and*, and *so on*. They will also need explicit and direct instruction in the vocabulary of the classroom. This includes words frequently used in giving instructions, words associated with subject areas, high-frequency words used in speech and texts, and all vocabulary necessary to understand a text. Whenever possible, vocabulary should be taught explicitly and backed up with images or objects.

- **comprehension:** Comprehension must be carefully scaffolded in a variety of ways. Teachers should provide as much background knowledge as possible to students who are unfamiliar with aspects of American culture. ELLs, like developing readers, are better able

to comprehend texts with low complexity. Such texts should be used to build comprehension skills. Graphic organizers, visual aids, and films or multimedia elements to promote comprehension may also be helpful.

- **cultural sensitivity:** Awareness of cultural differences is important for all students. It is especially relevant for English language learners, who may be unfamiliar with elements of American culture that many people take for granted. Assumptions about religious beliefs, dietary preferences, clothing choices, family structures, and so on should be avoided. Teachers should select a variety of texts and curricular resources to promote an understanding of diverse cultural perspectives. While many publishers now promote multicultural awareness, teachers should consider curricular resources that include diverse authorial voices.

Practice Question

8) A teacher is trying to make her unit on Shakespeare more accessible to English language learners. What is the BEST suggestion to help the teacher accomplish this?

- A. provide an alternate dramatic text on a different topic for ELL students to read

- B. encourage ELL students to use context clues as they read the play to identify new vocabulary

- C. pre-teach important roots and affixes to ELL students to aid in their decoding of new words in the play

- D. give ELL students a list of words and their definitions that are used frequently in the play

High-Achieving Students

While strategies are frequently offered for students with reading difficulties, there are also students who need greater challenges. As part of the Universal Design for Learning, all classrooms should use an approach that meets the needs of *all* learners and allows *all* students to access the same curriculum. Teachers can meet the needs of high-achieving students with a pyramid approach to plan lessons, as shown in Figure 7.3.

The UDL Planning Pyramid

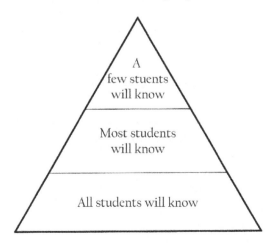

Figure 7.3. Universal Design for Learning Planning Pyramid

Another widely used model for advanced learners is **Renzulli's Enrichment Triad Model**. This model encourages three types of learning experiences:

1. exploratory opportunities

2. learning experiences in which thinking processes are developed

3. investigative activities

In this model, students typically have some sort of authentic experience with a topic. For example, they might take a field trip to visit a working farm and are then instructed on how to research and prepare a multimedia presentation on agriculture in the local community. This empowers the students to investigate agriculture in the community and prepare a multimedia presentation.

The following are ways to encourage a love of reading and a deeper exploration of texts by advanced readers in the classroom:

- Encourage choice of texts. Some students may be ready for more complex texts that are above the Lexile measure for their grade level. These students may find books or passages at grade level boring or redundant. Allowing advanced readers to choose their own materials can encourage them to explore topics of interest and increase engagement. Of course, educators should consider students' reading capabilities and socio-emotional development. Some of the more complex texts contain mature themes or subject matter that may not be appropriate for younger readers.

- Allow for appropriate pacing. Some students may benefit from **acceleration**, or moving through the curriculum at a faster rate than their peers. **Curriculum compacting** allows students who have already mastered parts of the curriculum to skip those areas and move on to new material.

- Extend learning through independent projects, project-based learning, or other methods that encourage critical thinking and a deeper comprehension of texts.

Independent learning is an appropriate enrichment activity for advanced readers, but it does not replace explicit instruction, from which high-achieving students also benefit. Advanced learners should not be given "busy work" or simply be given the entire class period for independent reading.

Teachers are encouraged to work with reading specialists to devise enrichment activities that extend *purposeful* learning and enhance the core curriculum. Such activities allow for student choice and exploration of individual interests.

Practice Question

9) Why would an assignment in which students select a story and then create a picture presentation summarizing its plot be appropriate for advanced readers?

    A. because it allows for student choice

    B. because it includes elements of technology

    C. because it makes use of curriculum compacting

    D. because it promotes homogenous grouping

Answer Key

1) D: Specially designed instruction is provided as part of an IEP but not under a 504 plan.

2) C: Specific comprehension deficits commonly co-occur in students with ASD.

3) C: This assessment measure would not identify students at risk for reading difficulties; it is not sensitive enough. Many students can write the letters but might not, for example, know the sound each letter corresponds with.

4) C: Access to an audio recording of the book will help the student feel less overwhelmed and also scaffold comprehension, as the focus is on listening skills versus reading skills.

5) B: Lucia is using language chunking and song lyrics to build vocabulary. These are features of early production.

6) A: In code-switching, students mix words from their first language in when they speak their second language.

7) B: This is a crucial piece of information since ELLs may have experienced disruptions or delays in schooling due to their journey to the United States.

8) D: Common Shakespearean words like "thine," "thou," and so on may be new to ELLs. They should be concretely defined before the students read the play.

9) A: Research indicates that student choice of reading material is a particularly effective strategy for advanced readers.

8. Assessment and Instructional Decision-Making

Measurement Concepts

Assessment is the process of gathering information from multiple sources to understand what students know. It also measures how students are progressing and if any problems have arisen in their development. Assessment of student learning and progress in reading is ongoing and should occur every school day.

Assessments are conducted in many areas of development, including cognitive, socio-emotional, and physical. Assessments can be used for a variety of purposes:

- identifying developmental delays
- evaluating student mastery of learning objectives
- designing appropriate interventions
- gauging the efficacy of program delivery
- determining the placements of students within programs

Data from assessments can then be used to make decisions. These decisions might be related to an individual student, a classroom, or even an entire school or district. Much educational research relies on assessment to yield data that can be applied broadly in other educational situations.

Assessments are ranked based on two factors: reliability and validity. **Reliability** is the rate at which the assessment produces the same outcome every time. One way to think about reliability is in terms of consistency across many different test takers and testing scenarios. A test has low reliability if it does not produce accurate results each time it is given.

Ideally, each assessment would give the same results, even when administered multiple times to the same student under the same conditions. Unfortunately, this is not the case. Even assessments that are thought to be reliable have measurement error. **Measurement error** refers to all the variations that impact an examinee's performance. Some variations are testing conditions (e.g., quietness of the room, behavior of the test administrator) or the emotional state of the test taker. Assessments of very young children often have significant measurement error compared to those of older children.

Additionally, many reading assessments conducted in English may contain errors or be ineffective when used with students with limited English proficiency. Particular attention should be paid to matching the assessment to the student needs and intended purpose.

Validity is quite different from reliability. It refers to whether the findings that the assessment instrument seeks to measure are accurate and backed by research and evidence. If the assessment does not measure

what it is supposed to measure (achievement, personality, intelligence, or something else), then it lacks validity even if it is reliable and produces consistent results each time.

Assessment data is generally quantitative (i.e., numerical) and qualitative (i.e., nonnumerical). **Quantitative** data is gleaned

> **Study Tip:**
>
> Use the roots of the words to remember quantitative and qualitative data. *Quant*itative data is a quantity. *Qual*itative data is the quality of something.

> **Study Tip:**
>
> Think of the concept of test reliability as you would a person who is reliable. A *reliable* person behaves as expected every time; a *reliable* assessment instrument does too.

from standardized assessments, such as a numerical IQ or performance in the fifteenth percentile. **Qualitative** data is usually obtained through interviews with parents and teachers and observational records. Both types of data should be considered in initial evaluation for reading interventions or special education services and in the ongoing assessment of student learning.

Practice Question

1) A teacher gives a published, criterion-referenced reading assessment instrument to a third-grade student on two different occasions within a week. The student scores much higher on the first assessment. This assessment has measurement error as well as which of the following?

A. reliability issues

B. validity issues

C. a biased norming group

D. a small norming group

Standardized Assessments

There are numerous **standardized** published assessment instruments. These instruments have standardized questions or criteria and are administered in a consistent manner. Most professionals agree that standardized assessments reveal only one part of any student's learning situation and level of mastery of individual objectives. Standardized assessments provide one way to gather data to help with individualized planning and instruction.

Norm-Referenced Assessments

Standardized assessments fall into two categories: norm-referenced and criterion-referenced. **Norm-referenced assessments** measure an individual student against a group of other test takers, typically those of the same age or grade level. Results are reported in a percentile ranking. These tests are most often used to measure achievement, intelligence, aptitude, and personality.

Achievement tests measure which skills a student has mastered. These tests often fall under categories such as reading and mathematics. Achievement tests are generally multiple-choice and require test takers to answer a standardized set of questions. Popular achievement tests include the following:

- the Iowa Test of Basic Skills (ITBS)
- the Peabody Individual Achievement Test
- the Wechsler Individual Achievement Test (WIAT-III)
- the Stanford Achievement Test

Intelligence tests are another norm-referenced assessment. They are used to measure overall intellectual functioning, problem-solving skills, and aptitude for learning. The following are the most commonly used intelligence tests:

- Stanford-Binet Intelligence Scales (SB5)
- Wechsler Intelligence Scale for Children (WISC-V)
- Woodcock-Johnson III Tests of Cognitive Abilities
- Differential Ability Scales (DAS-II)
- Universal Nonverbal Intelligence Test (for students with certain communication disorders)

Intelligence tests can help determine giftedness in children as well as the presence of intellectual disabilities. Intelligence tests are also used in tandem with achievement tests to note patterns or discrepancies in IQ and academic achievement. These discrepancies may be the result of specific learning disabilities or other conditions that might require special services.

> **Did You Know?**
>
> The first exams offered by the College Board (which now produces the SAT) were administered in 1901. The sections were English, French, German, Latin, Greek, history, mathematics, chemistry, and physics. Instead of the multiple-choice format of most of today's standardized tests, questions were in essay format. Student responses were graded as very poor, poor, doubtful, good, and excellent.

Because norm-referenced tests compare students to one another, the results must be given in a format that makes such a comparison possible. The most common way to do this is the percentile. A **percentile** is a score that shows where a student ranks in comparison to ninety-nine other students. For example, a percentile of 81 would mean that the student in question has performed equal to or outperformed eighty-one out of the other ninety-nine students who took the same test. A percentile of 14 means that the student only performed equal to or outperformed fourteen of the other ninety-nine test takers.

These percentiles are usually determined early in the development of a standardized norm-referenced assessment by using an early group of test takers known as a **norming group**. Depending on the assessment instrument, these norming groups may be students in a particular school (school average norm) or district (local norm group). They may also be students with particular diagnosed exceptionalities or special learning situations (special norm group). More often, the groups are national norm groups. These groups are carefully selected to be representative of the nation as a whole. One criticism of norm-referenced tests is that national norm groups are not always current and truly representative. For example, students might be taking a test that has not been recently recalibrated with a new norming group.

Norm-referenced tests base their percentiles on the bell-shaped curve, also called the normal curve or the normal distribution. Tests are often modified so that the results will generate a bell-shaped curve (Figure 8.1.). This distribution of scores has three primary characteristics:

- It is symmetrical from left to right.
- The mean, median, and mode are the same score and are at the center of the symmetrical distribution.
- The percentage within each standard deviation is known.

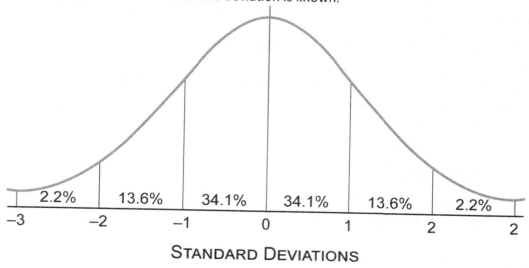

Figure 8.1. Bell-Shaped Curve (normal distribution)

Not all standardized assessment instruments use percentiles. There are also **grade-equivalent scores**, which provide a result in a grade level. This means that the student's performance is equal to the median performance corresponding to other students of a certain grade level. For example, if a student scores at a tenth-grade reading level, it would mean that the student's score was the same as the median for all tenth graders who took the test. Some assessment instruments also use age-equivalent scores, which simply compare a student's results to the median score of other students of a certain age.

Practice Question

2) Harvey scores in the 89th percentile on the Stanford Achievement Test, an annual norm-referenced test. What do these results mean?

   A. He got 89 percent of the questions correct.

   B. Eighty-nine percent of students did the same as or better than Harvey.

   C. Harvey did the same as or better than 89 percent of students.

   D. Harvey did well enough to be part of the norming group.

Criterion-Referenced Tests

Criterion-referenced tests measure an individual's performance as it relates to predetermined benchmarks or criteria. These tests are generally used to measure a student's progress toward meeting certain objectives. They do not compare test takers to one another but rather compare student knowledge against the set criteria. Criterion-referenced tests include everything from annual state tests to those created by teachers or educational publishers to assess the mastery of learning objectives.

One new incarnation of the criterion-referenced test used by many states is **standards-referenced testing**, or **standards-based assessment**. These tests measure a student's performance against certain content standards as defined by each grade level and subject. They are typically scored in categories such as basic, proficient, and advanced; or unsatisfactory, satisfactory, and advanced. Most annual state accountability tests, such as STAAR, PARCC, and many others, are standards-based, criterion-referenced tests.

Practice Question

3) A teacher wants to use the class-wide results of a criterion-referenced test as a starting point to identify levels of vocabulary knowledge among students. Which assessment results should the teacher reference?

- A. Iowa Test of Basic Skills
- B. annual state accountability test
- C. results from a phonics screener
- D. results from running records

Other Types of Assessments

Formal and Informal Assessments

Most programs try to maintain a balance between formal and informal assessment measures. **Formal assessments** refer to test results that are reported in either a percentile or percentage format. Standardized tests, chapter or unit tests, and end-of-course exams are all examples of formal assessments.

Informal assessments evaluate students outside the traditional written test format. These assessments help give more complete pictures of ongoing progress. At times, particularly when students experience stress in high-stakes testing scenarios, informal assessments might provide more accurate results.

Informal assessments include observation, portfolios, projects, presentations, and oral checks, among others. Informal assessment should be ongoing and guide instruction alongside formal assessments. Popular informal assessments in terms of student literacy development include the following:

- oral reading checks
- oral comprehension checks
- running records
- phonics screeners
- exit tickets
- informal writing assignments/journaling

Another popular informal reading assessment is the **Informal Reading Inventory (IRI)**. This assessment includes a word list to determine which level of the assessment should be given. It also features oral reading and silent reading portions. The assessment pinpoints the independent, instructional, and frustrational reading levels for each student. The results can then be used to differentiate instruction and choose appropriate reading material for the reading levels of each student.

Both formal and informal assessments can be used to gather information and guide instruction. Some students, however, simply do not perform well on formal assessments or may have test anxiety. In these instances, informal assessments are often better measures of student knowledge.

Practice Question

4) A teacher wants to assess student retainment of skills at the end of a small-group intervention aimed at vocabulary acquisition. Which method of assessment should the teacher use?

   A. administer a norm-referenced assessment

   B. ask students to write down three new words they learned

   C. ask students to write three words with long vowel sounds

   D. administer a standardized achievement test

Formative and Summative Assessments

Assessments—whether formal, informal, authentic, or more traditional—can also be either formative or summative. **Formative assessment** refers to the ongoing monitoring of student progress toward learning objectives. Formative assessments are often informal assessments whereby teachers seek more information to streamline instruction. For example, a kindergarten teacher may give frequent formative assessments by asking each student to read words from a sight word list or consonant blend chart. This will help the teacher determine each student's progress in learning to read. It will also provide appropriate and targeted instruction in areas where there is the most need.

> **Study Tip:**
>
> Formative assessments are used while students are *forming* their knowledge. Summative assessments are used to add up all of student learning into one lump *sum*.

Formative assessments can also be more formal. Examples include a short quiz over the day's material or a concept map or outline that students submit for grading. However, formative assessment tends to be low-stakes (i.e., does not carry a high point value). Formative assessment does not significantly impact a student's course grade or chances of promotion to the next grade.

Summative assessment is designed to evaluate student learning after the end of a defined unit of study. It compares student knowledge to the initial learning objectives that were addressed throughout the unit of study. It, too, may be formal or informal but may often take the form of a unit test, midterm or final exam, or a final paper or project. Summative assessments are generally high-stakes assessments because they carry high point values. They are often critical to students' overall grades and their ability to pass a course or be promoted to the next grade.

A middle ground between a formative assessment and a summative assessment is the **benchmark assessment**. This type of assessment is more formal than a formative assessment but is not a high-stakes standardized summative

> **Check Your Understanding:**
>
> Some districts give benchmark tests up to ten times a year, which has led to some state lawmakers limiting the number of benchmark assessments that can be given each year in the hopes of decreasing testing time and increasing instructional time. Does such a law exist in California?

assessment. Benchmark assessments are sometimes called interim assessments, or predictive assessments. They track student progress and determine the degree to which students are on track to perform well on future summative assessments.

Many states use benchmark assessments before the annual standards-based assessment in order to determine which students need interventions to help prepare for high-stakes tests. Benchmark assessments can also be used to evaluate overall school or district goals and whether or not the school or district is on track to achieve those goals.

In some cases, benchmark assessments are less formal. For example, a first-grade teacher using a leveled-reader program may employ a benchmark assessment to determine when her students are ready to move to the program's next level. Similarly, a kindergarten teacher whose goal is to have his students know all of the Dolch sight words might give them benchmark assessments over smaller sections of the list.

Practice Question

5) A reading teacher gives a daily warm-up quiz with a low point value that covers some of the material discussed the day before. Which type of assessment is he giving?

A. a benchmark assessment

B. a low-stakes formative assessment

C. a norm-referenced assessment

D. a high-stakes summative assessment

Authentic Assessments

One important trend in student assessment is authentic assessment. **Authentic assessment** measures the student's ability to use knowledge in a direct, relevant, often real-world way.

In an authentic literacy assessment, students apply reading and writing skills in pragmatic or practical ways. For example, high school students might work on writing a resume or a profile on a professional networking platform. These are both examples of an authentic assessment of skills in writing for a formal audience. Another example would be a fifth-grade teacher who might give students brochures for places to explore on a field trip and ask them to read and summarize the high points of each brochure. These are examples of authentic literacy assessments since they measure literacy skills in pragmatic contexts.

Authentic assessments offer opportunities to go much deeper than traditional written tests. There are numerous examples, many of them cross-curricular, that can be used to assess reading and writing skills in authentic contexts. Teachers across multiple disciplines can collaborate to design projects that assess multiple skills. For example, a science teacher and an English teacher might work together to have students research and summarize a scientific article to earn a grade for English and then design an experiment based on the article for a grade in science.

Practice Question

6) A fifth-grade teacher wants to create an authentic assessment to evaluate students' skills with writing in coherent paragraphs. Which assignment would BEST accomplish this goal?

    A. directing students to give a presentation to the class on something they know how to do well

    B. asking students to analyze the way paragraphs are used in a newspaper article on a topic of their choice

    C. assigning students to write the draft of an email they will eventually send to someone

    D. having students use a graphic organizer to organize their thoughts into paragraphs before writing an essay about an assigned topic

Diagnostic Assessments

Diagnostic assessments are used to determine what students already know. Many teachers give diagnostic assessments at the beginning of the school year or before each unit of study. This helps calibrate the level of instruction and can help track progress over time when diagnostic assessments are compared with summative assessments.

Diagnostic assessments are particularly important when teachers are implementing pyramid planning as part of the Universal Design for Learning (UDL). For example, if a teacher discovers through a diagnostic assessment that most of her first-grade students do not know all of the letter sounds, it would be unreasonable to expect all of her students to be reading sentences by the end of the first unit of study.

Diagnostic assessments can uncover learning gaps that teachers will need to address. For example, a second-grade teacher discovers that many of his students lack knowledge of long vowel sounds. This teacher will need to give explicit instruction on that topic before presenting a unit on spelling that requires students to drop the *e* and add a suffix.

Diagnostic assessments can also be used at the beginning of the year to identify students who are at risk of not meeting reading learning objectives and to differentiate instruction and plan interventions for these students. Meeting each student at their current learning situation is important in setting goals and targeting instruction.

Practice Question

7) Mrs. El-Badawi is a kindergarten teacher who wants to find out her students' level of phonemic awareness at the beginning of the school year so she can target her instruction. Which is the BEST type of assessment to accomplish this goal?

    A. a formative assessment

    B. a diagnostic assessment

    C. a summative assessment

    D. a play-based assessment

Peer, Self-, and Multi-Perspective Assessments

Teachers and parents are not the only ones who can participate in student assessments. Peers can also be very helpful in providing feedback on student learning. **Peer assessment** is the assessment of student work by peers.

Peer assessment is widely used in higher education, particularly in large online classes in which instructors are unable to give feedback on each student's work. If students receive appropriate guidance and practice, peer assessment can be used effectively in many secondary and even some elementary classrooms. While most peer assessments will not result in formal grades, they can be invaluable when it comes to helping students revise their work before submitting it for grading.

In a peer assessment, students are given a rubric or list of criteria and asked to assess another student's work based on this rubric or set of criteria. They are also asked to offer specific feedback for improvement. This process can help students who are unsure of how to revise or edit their work, as they are given clear and actionable suggestions.

Peer assessment can also be used during collaborative learning. In this model, the teacher asks for feedback from the group about the level of each member's participation. This can be particularly helpful if much of a group project happened outside of school. This way, the teacher can get some idea of each group member's contributions. This type of assessment is usually more effective when clear criteria for evaluation are set. The teacher might, for example, ask group members to fill out a chart showing which parts of the project each member completed individually and which parts were completed together.

Multi-perspective assessments are also used during cooperative learning activities. With these types of assessments, peers, the individual student, and teachers all collaborate to assess learning outcomes. This can be helpful when parts of a group project occur both in and out of the classroom. In this type of assessment, the teacher may weigh input from various assessors differently when computing the total overall grade. For example, the teacher evaluation of the finished project may count for 75 percent of the grade, the peer assessment of group members for another 10 percent, and the student's self-assessment for the remaining 15 percent.

> ### Did You Know?
>
> Any comprehensive evaluation for special education services will be multi-perspective since a multidisciplinary team, alongside a child's parents, will be participating in the process.

Peer assessment and multi-perspective assessment can be used in conjunction with self-assessment. **Self-assessment** is a student's evaluation of her individual progress toward learning goals. Self-assessment is a critical part of any child's overall education. It helps students become self-directed learners who devise and meet learning goals with little help from others. Self-assessment should be a large part of formative assessment. Students who are self-assessing can actively seek out the resources they need to meet learning objectives without waiting for teachers to realize they need them.

Usually, self-assessment must be explicitly taught. There are many strategies for this. Often, students are given an example of work that meets certain criteria and then asked to compare their work to this example. In other cases, students are asked to simply assess their degree of understanding of a concept. This could be anything from having students respond in journals or interactive notebooks to prompts such

as "Today I learned..." or "I am still unsure about..." Students might use simple symbols, like checkmarks or a happy/sad faces to indicate their degree of mastery of given concepts.

Practice Question

8) After a group project–based learning assignment, a reading teacher asks each group member to fill out an evaluation of their team members. Which method of assessment is this?

 A. peer assessment

 B. multi-perspective assessment

 C. self-assessment

 D. formative assessment

Assessing Emerging Readers

Students who are not yet fluent readers will need specific assessment techniques to ensure they are mastering foundational skills that form the building blocks of later reading instruction. Since concepts of print are the first stage of reading development, these skills must be mastered thoroughly. Most of the time, these assessments are informal and might include any of the following:

- asking students to point to the parts of a book (e.g., title, front cover, back)
- presenting students with a book and observing as they interact with it
- asking students to point to a word, sentence, or picture

As students progress to developing phonetic awareness or overall phonemic awareness, assessment is also conducted in a highly interactive manner. Students might be asked to clap out sounds or words, think of rhyming words, repeat words or sounds, and so on.

Once students begin to work on letter recognition and sound-symbol knowledge, letter charts or letter-sound charts can be used as assessment tools. Students can cross off each letter or letter sound once it is mastered. The same assessment method with a chart or list can be used for sight words (often with a Dolch word list), consonant blends, digraphs, diphthongs, and other challenging sounds.

There is an important distinction between children's ability to sing the alphabet song or point to and say letters or sounds in order (which many master quite early) and the different (though related) skill of letter and letter-sound recognition in isolation. For this reason, it is a good idea to always assess phonics skills in different contexts. For example, students can be asked to point to certain letters or sounds (/b/, /ch/, /i/) in a book or story. This type of **embedded phonics** assessment ensures that students can transfer knowledge and apply it in connected texts.

In addition to more structured assessment methods, like charts and lists, phonics skills can be assessed through any number of hands-on activities. Students can play with letter/sound cards or magnets and form or dissect words. Students can match up cards with different rimes and onsets or different target consonant or vowel sounds.

In assessing decoding, or the ability to sound out a word and glean meaning, an oral assessment approach continues to be the gold standard. There are many assessment tools designed specifically to aid in

assessing such skills, including the popular **Quick Phonics Screener**, which assesses a student's ability to read a variety of sounds and words.

When assessing decoding skills, it is important to note student strengths and weaknesses; however, teachers must also develop a general idea of a student's overall approach and "word-attack skills," or methods of decoding unfamiliar words. Attention to how students approach any oral reading task can provide significant information on strategies they are already using, as well as those they do not use but might find beneficial. Though the age of the student certainly comes into play, sometimes older students still mastering decoding might be able to verbalize the way they approach such challenging words. Questions posed to the student about strategy or method can also yield valuable information.

In addition to these methods, there are also several published assessment instruments for pre-readers and emerging readers:

- Letter knowledge and phonemic awareness can be assessed using the Dynamic Indicators of Basic Early Literacy Skills (DIBELS) and the Early Reading Diagnostic Assessment (ERDA).

- The Comprehensive Test of Phonological Processing (CTOPP) and Phonological Awareness Test (PAT) can also be used as instruments to assess phonemic awareness.

- Other instruments that assess early reading skills include the Texas Primary Reading Inventory (TPRI), Test of Word Reading Efficiency (TOWRE), and even the kindergarten version of the Iowa Test of Basic Skills (ITSB).

Regardless of the assessment instruments used, assessing emerging readers can be challenging since young children often find assessment scenarios intimidating. Any single assessment is only as useful the portion of the full picture that it provides. The fullest picture of a student's pre-reading development can best be gleaned through observation and input from both parents and teachers. Portfolios, observational records, checklists, and other informal assessment methods can provide much insight into the development of emergent readers.

Practice Question

9) A kindergarten teacher who wants to assess student mastery of phoneme blending would MOST likely do which of the following?

A. ask students to add affixes to various root words

B. have students match up cards with onsets and rimes and say each word

C. ask students to remove a letter from a word, add a new one, and read the new word

D. have students point to items in the classroom that begin with a certain letter sound

Assessing Reading Skills and Strategies

Assessing each student in an individual oral context is not always possible. This can make assessing reading skills and metacognitive reading strategies a challenge. Furthermore, it is often hard to fully assess any one student's individual thought process. With these caveats, assessing reading skills and strategies with an eye for gaps that might be addressed through intervention is an important task.

Word-attack skills can be assessed through observation and oral reading. Teachers should take note of what happens when students encounter words they do not know. Do they immediately ask for help? Do they skip over the word? Do they reread the word? Do they slow down or speed up? Assessing word-attack skills relies on observing students as they read aloud but also on assessing the underlying skills that lead to a strong word-attack tool kit. Do students make use of all text features and graphic elements? Do they sound out the word or make inferences based on roots and affixes? Do they use context clues?

Vocabulary assessment typically happens in the context of **breadth** (the number of words one knows) or **depth** (the ability to use the vocabulary in varied and nuanced ways). It also happens in the context of an isolated assessment (a vocabulary test) or as an embedded assessment as an adjunct to another assessment, such as one of reading comprehension or oral fluency.

Such assessments can also be context-independent: "What does *contortion* mean?" or context-dependent: "What does the word *contort* mean in the following sentence?" Educators should consider what "bank" they will draw vocabulary from in order to assess students. Typically, teachers assess the vocabulary that students will need in order to comprehend the language of classroom instruction, the textbook, and any literature the class will read. Reference materials such as the *EDL Core Vocabularies* define "target" words per grade level. Published standardized vocabulary instruments, such as the classic **Peabody Picture Vocabulary Test (PPT)**, which requires no reading or writing, can also be used to assess individual students.

Assessing oral fluency is generally done by assessing reading accuracy, prosody, and automaticity. This can be tracked in numerous ways. Teachers may keep **running records** (Figure 8.2.)that track accuracy, self-correction, and the use of fix-up strategies and word-attack skills. Running records use forms so teachers can mark errors, self-corrections, and how students use cues to make meaning of texts. These forms are filled out as the student reads the same text the teacher has.

Oral fluency can also be tracked using digital tools, such as collecting and analyzing recordings of students reading aloud.

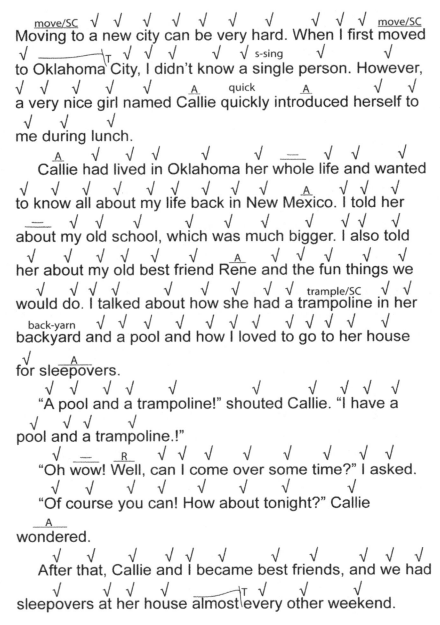

Figure 8.2. Running Record

Students can also be measured for oral reading skills using various fluency norms charts that indicate average words read correctly per minute per grade. While several standard measures exist, one of the most researched is the **Hasbrouck-Tindal oral reading fluency chart**. This chart measures progress over the course of the school year and from grade to grade. It compares students in percentiles with their peers on a scale of words read correctly per minute.

Table 8.1. Hasbrouck-Tindal Oral Reading Fluency Chart			
Words Correct Per Minute (50th percentile)			
Grade	Fall	Winter	Spring
1	---	29	60
2	50	84	100
3	83	97	112
4	94	120	133
5	121	133	146
6	132	145	146

Comprehension while reading silently can be assessed through **cloze exercises**. In these exercises, words are removed from the text and students must fill them in. There are other written exercises aimed at determining comprehension levels. Some students might struggle to answer written questions; therefore, a full assessment of silent reading comprehension should include an oral component as well.

As previously mentioned, one of the most common assessments is the Informal Reading Inventory (IRI). There are multiple versions created by various entities. One of the more popular versions is **Pearson's Qualitative Reading Inventory (QRI)**. These assessments include oral reading of word lists that assess the accuracy of word identification. The QRI also contains passages and questions that assess both oral and silent reading comprehension. Standardized norm-referenced test batteries, such as the Iowa Test of Basic Skills and Stanford Achievement Test, as well as several criterion-referenced tests, such as the Partnership for Assessment of Readiness for College and Careers (PARCC), also test reading comprehension.

Another popular assessment instrument is called Star. Often used for benchmark data (to see how students are progressing toward meeting objectives), this computer-based assessment includes a built-in tracking and analysis system to help teachers and schools identify students in need of additional support.

However, as in all types of reading assessment, comprehension assessment does not require a lengthy formal written test. Simply asking students to recount or retell a story they have read or to recall the most important or interesting parts of a text can provide valuable data. Furthermore, self-assessment should be ongoing and explicitly taught to all readers in order to monitor comprehension. As students self-assess, they can apply fix-up or fix-it-up strategies as needed when comprehension breaks down.

Practice Question

10) A reading teacher asks students to skim the text and turn the bold paragraph headings into questions. After the students have read the text silently, the teacher asks them to write answers to each of the questions. Which skill is the teacher assessing?

- A. identifying tone
- B. recalling main ideas
- C. activating background knowledge
- D. making inferences

Using Assessment Data

Data from reading assessments can be used in many ways. In schools using a **Multi-Tiered Systems of Support (MTSS)** framework, all students should be screened for reading proficiency early and often. Ongoing assessment (progress monitoring) should be implemented as reading interventions occur.

In an MTSS framework, teachers may conduct universal screenings with any number of assessment tools and then determine which students would benefit from interventions. This data can then be used to determine goals for students identified as "at risk" of not meeting reading objectives. These students will receive early intervening services (Tier 2 intervention) through many possible avenues, though small-group reading instruction is the most common.

As these Tier 2 interventions occur, the teacher and/or interventionist will continue to monitor progress and use assessment data to determine if the student is responding or needs more intensive intervention (Tier 3). This type of intervention is usually in a smaller group and of a greater frequency and longer duration.

When reading teachers are working as co-teachers or as direct providers of intervention services, they will also use assessment for the following purposes:

- to differentiate instruction for all students (Tier 1 interventions), including but not limited to
  - assessing the independent, instructional, and frustrational reading levels for each student and selecting appropriate texts;
  - providing scaffolds and supports for individual students per the principles of the Universal Design for Learning (UDL); and
  - using data for flexible grouping strategies that group students by skill level for optimal instruction but constantly reassess and adapt based on student progress
- to plan and conduct small-group interventions (Tier 2 or Tier 3) by
  - assessing skill gaps where students need additional instruction or practice, and
  - grouping students for interventions based on similar instructional goals/learning needs (keeping in mind principles of flexible grouping)

Assessment data can—and should—also be used on a macro level to make improvements to instruction and support teachers across the content areas. A teacher might use reading assessment data in a variety of contexts:

- determining individual classrooms/grade levels that might need additional support

The Authority in Teacher Certification

- determining grade-level or school-wide curricular needs
- determining the efficacy of classroom/grade-level or school-wide curricular or intervention approaches
- designing intervention approaches or teacher support systems on a school-wide level
- recognizing trends across grade levels (e.g., students not adequately prepared for instruction on spelling words with *r*-controlled vowels at the beginning of second grade)
- providing planning or instructional recommendations to teachers
- identifying teachers or classrooms to serve as mentors
- planning topics for professional development events

The way in which assessment data is used on a school-wide level will vary, but the items listed above are some of the most common uses of such information.

Practice Question

11) After reviewing the data from annual standards-based assessments, a teacher sees that results show that most third- and fourth-grade students are struggling with the meaning of homographs. Which area of instruction would be BEST to focus on in order to aid students in determining the meaning of homographs?

    A. roots and affixes

    B. graphophonic cues

    C. context clues

    D. analogy-based phonics

Answer Key

1) A: Reliability refers to how often a test gives the same result. This test clearly has some issues with reliability, as the student should score with similar results on multiple assessments in a short time frame.

2) C: Harvey's score was equal to or better than 89 percent of students to whom he is being compared.

3) B: Most annual state accountability tests are standards-based assessments that are criterion-referenced based on state standards. These assessment results would help the reading interventionist phrase student needs in a concrete and standards-aligned way.

4) B: This is a short, informal assessment that gives the teacher the needed data about what has been retained from the session.

5) B: A daily warm-up quiz is a low-stakes formative assessment. It is designed to be an ongoing monitoring of student learning and has a low point value.

6) C: This assignment is considered an authentic assessment because students will actually send their emails to people, so the assessment has a real-world application. It also allows the teacher to assess the students' use of paragraphs.

7) B: A diagnostic assessment will help Mrs. El-Badawi determine her students' existing knowledge of phonemic awareness.

8) A: When students assess other students it is known as peer assessment.

9) B: When students say the onset and rime together, they are blending both phonemes.

10) B: The paragraph headings and the questions generated from them are clues to the main idea of each paragraph. Asking students to answer the questions requires them to recall main ideas from the text.

11) C: The context of the sentence in which the homograph is written will clue its meaning. Instruction in looking for context clues will aid students in determining the meaning of these types of multiple-meaning words.

LACTANCIA MATERNA

SIN COMPLICACIONES

TERCERA EDICIÓN REVISADA

AMY SPANGLER, MN, RN, IBCLC

Producción

Diseño: The Office of PlayLab, Inc., playlab.org, Brooklyn, Nueva York, EE. UU.
Portada y fotografía interior: Gary Sloan Studios, garysloan.com, Brooklyn, Nueva York, EE. UU.
Contraportada y fotografía interior: Jensen Larson Photography, jensenlarson.com, Orlando, Florida, EE. UU.
Ilustraciones: Rick Powell, Montpelier, Vermont, EE. UU.
Administración de la producción y edición: Health Communication Connection, Vienna, Virginia, EE. UU.
Impresión: Specialty Lithographing Co., Cincinnati, Ohio, EE. UU.
Traducción: TrueLanguage, LLC, truelanguage.com, Georgia, EE. UU.

15 14 13 12   1 2 3 4 5

ISBN 978-1-933634-38-8

A todas las familias

Aprender a dar el pecho es como aprender a andar en bicicleta; puede parecer difícil al principio, pero una vez que se aprende resulta muy sencillo.

Hay algunas cosas que necesitas saber antes de empezar...

Ten paciencia

Algunos bebés saben cómo amamantarse de inmediato, pero la mayoría necesitan aprender.

Sé persistente

Pueden pasar varios días o varias semanas antes de que tú y tu bebé sepan qué hacer.

Siéntete orgullosa

Le estás dando a tu bebé un obsequio que durará para siempre.

ÍNDICE

¡Encontrarás **videos** y **consejos importantes** a lo largo de todo este libro!

Los códigos QR, como el que se muestra en el recuadro a continuación, les permitirán a los usuarios de Smartphone ver videos extra de forma fácil en el sitio web de baby gooroo. ¿No tienes Smartphone? Simplemente visita la dirección web indicada.

 Consulta este video para obtener más información de la serie de videos baby gooroo. **babygooroo.com/video/intro/sp**

 Los elefantes comparten consejos importantes que no querrás olvidar. ¿Lista? ¡Adelante!

CAPÍTULO 1
LA DECISIÓN DE AMAMANTAR

¿Por qué debo dar el pecho?

La lactancia es la forma en la que se supone que todos los bebés deben alimentarse. Es la forma más segura y sencilla de alimentar a tu bebé y le facilita las cosas a toda la familia. Un bebé saludable y feliz hace que cada miembro de la familia se sienta orgulloso.

¡Los bebés que se amamantan son más saludables! Estos bebés tienen...

- menos infecciones de los oídos.
- menos gas, estreñimiento y diarrea.
- menor riesgo de pulmonía.
- menor riesgo de alergias y asma.
- menor riesgo de síndrome de muerte súbita infantil.
- menor riesgo de obesidad infantil.
- menor riesgo de diabetes.

¡Los bebés que se amamantan son más felices! Estos bebés...

- te llegan a conocer de inmediato.
- se sienten seguros en tus brazos.

¡Los bebés que se amamantan son más inteligentes! Los bebés que se amamantan...

- tienen mejor desarrollo cerebral.
- obtienen mejores resultados en las pruebas de coeficiente intelectual.

¡Las madres que dan el pecho son más saludables!
Estas madres tienen...

- menos sangrado después del parto y bajan de peso más rápido.
- menor riesgo de cáncer en los senos, los ovarios y el útero.
- huesos más resistentes.

La lactancia es la forma más segura y sencilla de alimentar a tu bebé.

¡La lactancia ahorra tiempo y dinero! Los padres de los bebés que se amamantan...

- ahorran más de $1,000 dólares tan solo durante el primer año al no tener que comprar equipo y fórmula.
- faltan menos días al trabajo.
- pierden menos ingresos.

¡Tu leche es el único alimento hecho especialmente para tu bebé! La leche materna...

- contiene más de 200 nutrientes.
- siempre está lista.
- es limpia y segura.
- nunca está demasiado caliente ni demasiado fría.
- hace que las vacunas funcionen mejor.

¡La lactancia hace que tu vida sea más fácil!

 Mamás y papás que comparten consejos acerca de la lactancia:
babygooroo.com/video/advice/sp

¿Qué debo hacer si mis familiares y amigos me dicen que no dé el pecho?

Mientras más sepas acerca de la lactancia, más fácil te será pasar por alto los comentarios de tus familiares y amigos que no te sean útiles. Comienza por aprender todo lo que puedas antes de que nazca tu bebé, y comparte esta información con las personas más cercanas a ti. Una vez que tus familiares y amigos entiendan las muchas formas en que la lactancia los beneficia a ti y a tu bebé, es posible que te den más apoyo. Hazles saber que respetas sus decisiones y que esperas que ellos respeten las tuyas. Por encima de todo, hazles saber que son una parte importante de tu vida y que esperas que también formen una parte importante de la vida de tu bebé.

¿Cómo puedo amamantar frente a otros sin sentirme incómoda?

Algunas madres se sienten incómodas al amamantar frente a otros, pero otras no se sienten así. Si vives en un lugar donde se considera que los senos son principalmente objetos sexuales, es posible que sientas timidez al amamantar cuando haya otras personas presentes. Quizás te ayude recordar que los senos están hechos para alimentar a los bebés. Con un poco de práctica, puedes aprender a dar el pecho sin exponer los senos. Hazle saber a tu compañero que necesitas su apoyo. ¡Ten confianza! Le estás dando lo mejor a tu bebé.

Mamás que comparten consejos acerca de cómo amamantar fuera de casa:
babygooroo.com/video/public/sp

Con un poco de práctica podrás aprender a dar el pecho
sin exponer los senos.

¿Se sentirá excluido mi compañero?

La lactancia beneficia a todos los que forman parte de la vida de tu bebé. Los bebés que se amamantan acuden menos al médico y al hospital por enfermedades, lo cual facilita la crianza de los hijos. Las tomas nocturnas son más fáciles cuando no es necesario mezclar, medir o calentar la fórmula. Los bebés que se amamantan son portátiles, lo cual es una buena noticia para las familias activas.

Dile a tu compañero cuánto necesitas su apoyo mientras aprendes a cuidar a tu bebé.

La lactancia requiere tiempo y energía, especialmente en las primeras semanas. Es fácil que los compañeros, especialmente los papás, se desanimen. Por fortuna, las primeras semanas pasan pronto. Dile a tu compañero cuánto necesitas su apoyo mientras aprendes a cuidar a tu bebé.

Consejos para los compañeros, especialmente los papás

- Aprende todo lo que puedas acerca de la lactancia.
- Ayuda a colocar al bebé, hacerlo eructar y cambiarle los pañales.
- Alimenta a tu compañera mientras ella alimenta a tu bebé.
- Hazle saber a tu compañera que estás orgulloso de ella.
- Pasa algo de tiempo a solas con tu bebé todos los días; llévalo a pasear, juega con él mientras lo bañas, cántale, baila, léele o simplemente siéntate a ver televisión con él.
- Si te sientes celoso o enojado, habla acerca de tus sentimientos.
- ¡Pasa algo de tiempo a solas con tu pareja cada semana!

Papás que hablan acerca de lo que significa tener un bebé que se amamanta:
babygooroo.com/video/dads/sp

¿Tengo los senos demasiado pequeños para amamantar?

Los senos vienen en todo tipo de formas y tamaños. Las mujeres que tienen los senos pequeños producen la misma cantidad de leche que las mujeres con senos grandes. La mayoría de los bebés aprenden a amamantar de los senos de su madre si les da la oportunidad. ¡Lo único que se requiere es práctica!

El tamaño y la forma del pezón pueden hacer que la lactancia sea más fácil o más difícil para algunos bebés. Si tienes preguntas acerca del tamaño o la forma de tus senos o pezones, habla con tu proveedor de atención para la salud.

¿Me cambiará el tamaño y la forma de los senos con la lactancia?

Existen varios factores que pueden hacer que cambie el tamaño y la forma de los senos, como la edad, el embarazo, los factores hereditarios y el aumento o pérdida de peso. Quizás descubras que tus senos se vuelven más pequeños después de que nazca el bebé y bajes el peso que aumentaste durante el embarazo. Esto puede suceder sin importar cómo decidas alimentar a tu bebé.

¿Dar el pecho duele?

Es posible que sientas un tirón, un jalón o dolor al principio de la toma cuando el bebé se prenda al seno. Si tu bebé está bien colocado, el dolor durará solo unos segundos. Si dura más

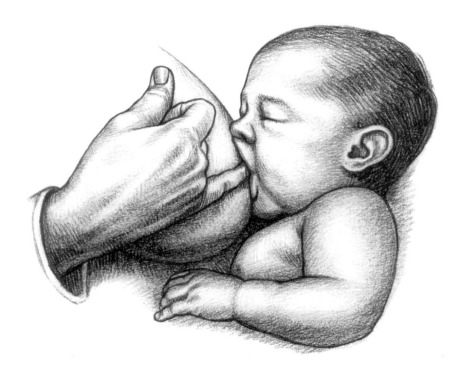

Interrumpe la succión deslizando un dedo
en el interior de la boca del bebé.

de unos segundos, interrumpe la succión deslizando un dedo en el interior de la boca del bebé. Retira al bebé del seno e inténtalo de nuevo.

 Mamás que comparten consejos acerca de cómo saber si el bebé está bien prendido: **babygooroo.com/video/latch/sp**

 ¡Ay! Algunas mamás sienten dolor cuando los bebés se prenden, pero esto debe durar solo unos segundos. Si el dolor continúa, interrumpe la succión deslizando un dedo en el interior de la boca del bebé. Retira al bebé del seno e inténtalo de nuevo.

CAPÍTULO 2
CÓMO PREPARARTE PARA AMAMANTAR

¿Cómo producen leche los senos?

El interior del seno contiene unos grupos de células con forma
de uvas que son las encargadas de producir la leche. Estas
células productoras de leche se llaman *alveolos*. Unos tubos
pequeños llamados *conductos de leche* transportan la leche
de los alveolos hasta los orificios del pezón. Los pequeños
bultos con apariencia de espinillas que se encuentran en la
areola, la parte más oscura del seno alrededor del pezón, se
llaman *glándulas de Montgomery*. Estas glándulas producen una
sustancia aceitosa que protege el pezón.

Cuando el bebé se amamanta, tu cerebro recibe el siguiente
mensaje: "¡Tengo hambre!" Tu cerebro escucha el mensaje y
le envía una señal a tus senos para que liberen la leche. Esta
liberación de leche se conoce como el *reflejo del chorro de leche*.
Es posible que tengas una sensación de cosquilleo o quemazón
en los senos cuando te baje la leche. O quizás veas que te gotea
leche de los pezones. No te preocupes si no sientes ni ves nada.
Cada mamá es diferente.

El cerebro también le envía señales a los senos para que
produzcan más leche para reemplazar la que toma el bebé.

 Mientras más leche tome tu bebé de tus senos,
más leche producirás.

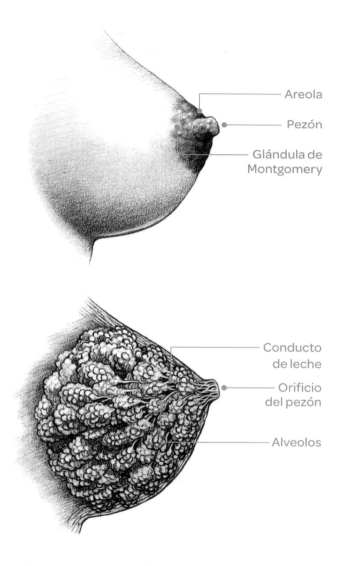

Areola

Pezón

Glándula de
Montgomery

Conducto
de leche

Orificio
del pezón

Alveolos

Los senos humanos tienen muchos componentes,
y cada uno de ellos tiene una función especial.

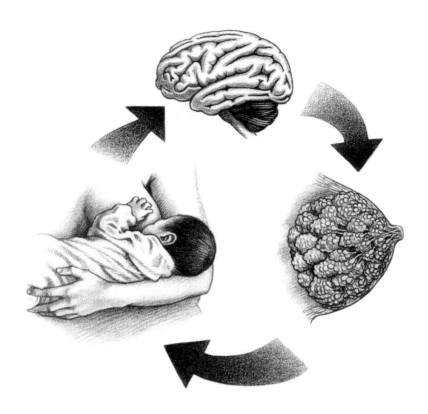

Para amamantar, lo único que necesitas tener
es un seno, un bebé y un cerebro.

¿Qué apariencia tiene la leche humana?

El *calostro* es la primera leche que producen los senos. Puede ser espesa y amarilla, o transparente y aguada. La producción del calostro puede comenzar a partir de la semana 16 del embarazo y continúa durante algunos días después del parto. Los bebés recién nacidos necesitan tomar pequeñas cantidades de alimento con frecuencia, así que las mamás producen cantidades pequeñas de calostro cada día. El calostro ayuda a que tu bebé haga popó, lo protege contra las enfermedades y le satisface el hambre y la sed. El calostro es la primera vacuna de tu bebé.

Durante las primeras 2 semanas después del parto, tu leche irá cambiando poco a poco hasta convertirse en leche madura. La leche madura tiene dos partes, la leche inicial y la leche final. La leche inicial es aguada y ligera. La leche final es espesa y cremosa. Tu bebé recibe la leche inicial al principio de la toma y la leche final se obtiene al final de la alimentación. La leche final contiene más cantidad de la grasa y las calorías que tu bebé necesita para crecer. Si limitas el tiempo de las tomas, tu bebé recibirá poco o nada de leche final.

El calostro se produce solo para los bebés recién nacidos, y proporciona todos los nutrientes que tu bebé necesita. Quizás no parezca leche, ¡pero sí lo es!

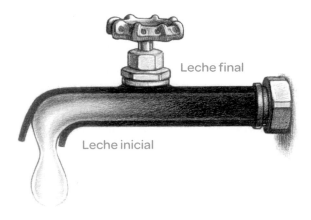

La leche inicial se obtiene al principio de la toma
y la leche final se obtiene al final de la alimentación.

¿Cómo me cuido los senos?

Los senos y los pezones casi no requieren cuidados. Las *glándulas de Montgomery*, que son pequeños bultos con forma de espinillas que se encuentran en la parte más oscura del seno, alrededor del pezón, producen una sustancia aceitosa. Esta sustancia ayuda a mantener humectados los pezones y los protege de las infecciones.

Cuando comiences a amamantar, sigue estas sencillas instrucciones...

- Lávate los senos una vez al día cuando te bañes.

- Utiliza solamente agua limpia y un jabón suave. No utilices lociones, cremas ni aceites.

- No es necesario que uses sostén mientras amamantas si no estás acostumbrada a usarlo. Sin embargo, si deseas utilizar un sostén por comodidad o soporte, quizás te sea útil usar un sostén para lactancia. Selecciona un sostén de algodón que se ajuste fácilmente y que te permita sentirte cómoda. Evita usar sostenes con varilla. Si prefieres un sostén con varilla, quítatelo para amamantar una o dos veces durante el día, así como durante la noche. Esto permitirá la extracción de leche de todas las partes del seno.

- Si necesitas usar protectores absorbentes dentro del sostén para proteger la ropa, recuerda cambiártelos con frecuencia. Selecciona protectores absorbentes hechos con capas suaves de algodón, seda o lana. No utilices protectores forrados de plástico que atrapen la humedad. Algunos protectores están hechos para usarse solamente una vez; otros se pueden lavar y usarse de nuevo.

- Si se te reseca la piel, puedes utilizar una pequeña cantidad de lanolina modificada. Con un poco es suficiente.

- Si te duelen los pezones, aplica unas gotas de leche materna al pezón y la areola después de cada toma.

- ¡Si tienes dolor, grietas o sangrado en los pezones, llama a tu proveedor de atención para la salud para que te ayude!

Evita el uso de lociones, cremas o aceites
en los senos y en los pezones.

CAPÍTULO 3
EL INICIO DE LA LACTANCIA

¿Cómo comienzo?

Las mamás y los bebés saben cómo lactar, ¡simplemente no sabes que lo sabes hasta que lo intentas! Aunque la lactancia parezca difícil al principio, una vez que aprendas será fácil.

La primera vez que amamantes a tu bebé

Coloca a tu bebé piel con piel entre tus senos por lo menos durante la primera hora después de su nacimiento. Los bebés nacen con sentidos y reflejos que les ayudan a oler, gatear, lamer, prenderse y amamantarse. ¡Es increíble!

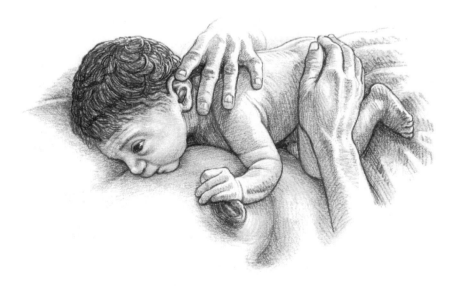

Coloca a tu bebé piel con piel entre tus senos al menos durante la primera hora después de su nacimiento.

Deja para después las tareas menos importantes como bañar y cambiarle el pañal al bebé, hasta que haya tenido la oportunidad de conocerte y amamantarse.

Las siguientes veces que amamantes a tu bebé

Mantén a tu bebé contigo día y noche. Esta es tu oportunidad de aprender a dar el pecho.

Busca las primeras señales de hambre, y ofrécele el seno en cuanto aparezcan. Las primeras señales de hambre incluyen los chasquidos con la boca, chuparse los dedos o los puños, retorcerse e inquietarse.

Elije una posición cómoda. Coloca a tu bebé sobre tu pecho, voltéalo para que quede sobre un costado o acomódalo bajo tu brazo de forma que la cabeza, los hombros, las rodillas y el pecho se encuentren frente a tu seno. Piensa cómo te colocas frente a la mesa para comer, y coloca a tu bebé de la misma forma.

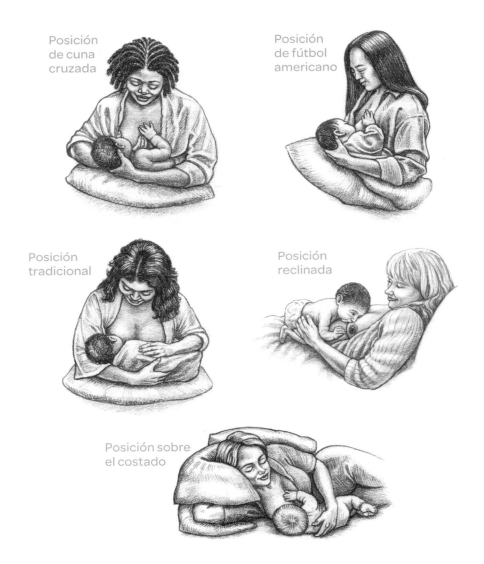

Posición de cuna cruzada

Posición de fútbol americano

Posición tradicional

Posición reclinada

Posición sobre el costado

Elije una posición cómoda. Piensa cómo te colocas frente a la mesa para comer, y coloca a tu bebé de la misma forma.

Sostén tu seno. Si necesitas sostenerte el seno con la mano, asegúrate de colocar los dedos alejados del pezón.

Sostén a tu bebé. Coloca el pulgar y los otros dedos debajo de las orejas y alrededor de la nuca de tu bebé para sostenerlo. No coloques la mano en la parte posterior de la cabeza del bebé.

Extrae (exprime) unas pocas gotas de calostro. Coloca el pulgar y los dedos en lados opuestos de la areola, que es la parte más oscura del seno alrededor del pezón. Presiona contra el pecho. Después comprime (exprime suavemente) el seno, no el pezón, entre el pulgar y los dedos.

Hazle cosquillas en la nariz a tu bebé con el pezón. Cuando abra bien la boca, como si estuviera bostezando, colócalo suavemente sobre el seno, comenzando con la barbilla y el labio inferior. ¡Asegúrate de que esté bien prendido y de que tenga la boca llena de seno!

 Mamás que comparten sugerencias acerca de cómo colocar a los bebés: babygooroo.com/video/positioning/sp

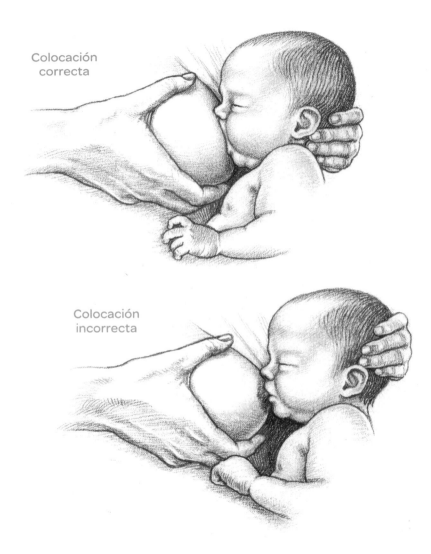

Colocación
correcta

Colocación
incorrecta

¡Asegúrate de que esté bien prendido y de que
tenga la boca llena de seno!

Mantén a tu bebé cerca de ti y en una posición cómoda. Si mantienes a tu bebé cerca, podrá prenderse bien y comprimir tu seno entre el paladar y la lengua.

Revisa la posición de la nariz, las mejillas, la barbilla y los labios de tu bebé. La barbilla de tu bebé debe estar firmemente presionada en tu seno. La nariz y las mejillas pueden tocar ligeramente el seno. ¡Debe tener la boca bien abierta como si estuviera bostezando, y los labios deben estar curvados hacia fuera como si fueran los labios de un pez!

¡Observa a tu bebé y olvídate del reloj! Amamanta a tu bebé todo el tiempo que él quiera en el primer seno antes de ofrecerle el otro (aproximadamente de 10 a 20 minutos). Cuando tu bebé deje de mamar y succionar o se quede dormido, despiértalo, hazlo eructar y ofrécele el otro seno.

Mamás que comparten consejos acerca de cómo saber si el bebé está bien prendido:
babygooroo.com/video/latch/sp

Interrumpe la succión antes de desprender al bebé del seno.
Puedes interrumpir la succión deslizando suavemente un dedo
entre las encías del bebé y hacia el interior de la boca.

Ofrécele ambos senos en cada alimentación, pero no te
preocupes si parece estar satisfecho después de tomar solo uno.

¡Observa a tu bebé y olvídate del reloj!

Comienza cada toma con el seno que le ofreciste la última vez.

Alimenta a tu bebé con frecuencia. El estómago de tu bebé es aproximadamente del mismo tamaño que su puño, así que lo mejor son las tomas pequeñas y frecuentes.

Evita los biberones y los chupones. Los biberones y los chupones pueden confundir a tu bebé. Espera hasta que tú y el bebé hayan aprendido a amamantar bien antes de ofrecerle un biberón o un chupón.

Evita los suplementos. Tu leche contiene todos los nutrientes que tu bebé necesita. Si le das agua, fórmula u otros alimentos a tu bebé, producirás menos leche.

¡Relájate y disfruta de estos momentos con tu bebé!

 Tu leche es el único alimento que tu bebé necesita durante aproximadamente los primeros 6 meses.

¿Con cuánta frecuencia debo amamantar?

Dale el pecho a tu bebé siempre que muestre señales de hambre o sed. Estas señales incluyen retorcerse, menearse, hacer chasquidos con la boca, chuparse las manos o los dedos, inquietarse y llorar.

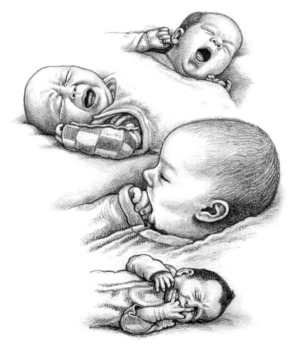

Las primeras señales para la alimentación incluyen los chasquidos con la boca, chuparse los dedos, retorcerse, inquietarse y bostezar.

Algunos bebés se amamantan en intervalos de 1 a 3 horas durante el día y la noche; otros se amamantan cada hora durante tres a cinco tomas, y después duermen durante 3 a 4 horas. Cada bebé es diferente.

Tu bebé necesita amamantarse por lo menos ocho veces cada 24 horas. Muchos bebés se amamantan de 10 a 12 veces al día.

A veces, un bebé somnoliento no quiere comer con suficiente frecuencia, y será necesario que lo despiertes. Durante las primeras 4 a 6 semanas, si tu bebé no se despierta para comer por lo menos ocho veces cada 24 horas, observa las primeras señales de hambre o de sueño ligero. Ofrécele el seno en estos momentos. Mientras más leche tome tu bebé, más leche producirás.

Consejos para despertar a un bebé somnoliento

- Siéntalo sobre tu regazo y háblale.
- Dale masaje en los pies y la espalda.
- Quítale el pañal.
- Límpiale las nalguitas con una toallita húmeda y fresca.

 Tu bebé necesita amamantarse por lo menos ocho veces cada 24 horas. Sin embargo, muchos bebés se amamantan de 10 a 12 veces al día.

¿Cuánto tiempo dura una toma?

Tu bebé te dará señales de que está satisfecho. ¡Así que observa a tu bebé y olvídate del reloj!

Las tomas pueden ser cortas, largas o regulares. Cada toma puede durar de 5 a 10 minutos o hasta una hora. ¡La duración de la toma dependerá de si tu bebé solo quiere un refrigerio o una comida completa!

Cuando tu bebé deje de mamar y tragar, hazlo eructar y ofrécele el otro seno. Si no se alimentó bien en el primer seno, colócalo de nuevo en el mismo seno antes de ofrecerle el segundo seno para asegurarte de que obtenga la grasa y las calorías que necesita para crecer. No te preocupes si se alimenta solo de un seno. ¡Cada uno de tus senos puede proporcionarle una comida completa!

Cada uno de tus senos puede proporcionarle una comida completa! Así que no te preocupes si el bebé se alimenta solo de un seno.

Tu bebé te dará señales de que está satisfecho.

¿Por qué la lactancia parece tan difícil al principio?

Existen diferentes factores que pueden afectar la rapidez con que la madre y el bebé aprenden a amamantar. Estos factores incluyen la edad del bebé, el uso de medicamentos para el dolor por parte de la madre durante el parto, el tipo de nacimiento (vaginal o por cesárea), la duración del parto, el uso de instrumentos durante el nacimiento (fórceps o extractor a vacío) y las infecciones o enfermedades de la madre o el bebé.

Incluso cuando la madre y el bebé están saludables, aprender a amamantar requiere tiempo y práctica. Las tomas frecuentes desde el principio les ayudarán a ti y a tu bebé a tener un buen inicio. La lactancia se facilitará a medida que tú y el bebé se vuelvan más fuertes. ¡En poco tiempo te será difícil recordar por qué la lactancia te pareció tan complicada alguna vez!

Mamás que comparten sus opiniones acerca de lo más difícil de la lactancia:
babygooroo.com/video/hardest/sp

Aprender a amamantar requiere paciencia y práctica.

CAPÍTULO 4
CÓMO CUIDAR A TU BEBÉ

¿Cómo puedo cuidar a mi bebé y hacer todas las cosas que necesito hacer?

Durante las primeras semanas después del nacimiento, tu labor más importante es cuidar a tu bebé y cuidarte a ti misma. Déjales las tareas del hogar a los demás, o si es necesario no las termines; ¡las telarañas pueden esperar!

Las frustraciones de la crianza de los hijos parecen ser mayores cuando los padres están agotados por falta de sueño. Así que trata de tomar siestas por lo menos una vez durante el día cuando tu bebé duerma, y usa tu piyama o camisón durante la primera semana como recordatorio para la familia y los amigos de que aún te estás recuperando.

Algunas madres se sienten cómodas al amamantar frente a sus familiares y amigos (tanto hombres como mujeres), pero otras no. Así que no dudes en decirles si sientes que necesitas más privacidad. Puedes limitar la cantidad de visitantes y la duración de las visitas colocando un pequeño letrero de "No molestar" en la puerta de tu casa.

Es bueno contar con ayuda en casa, pero los familiares y amigos pueden ser motivo de estrés. Es posible que tú o tu compañero tengan que explicarles amablemente los beneficios de la lactancia y la importancia de las tomas frecuentes, de la alimentación a solicitud y de las tomas durante la noche.

Explícales que es mejor para ti y para tu bebé tomar siestas durante el día y amamantar durante la noche, que hacer que la abuelita le dé el biberón a tu bebé para que tú puedas dormir toda la noche.

Come gran variedad de alimentos saludables y toma suficientes líquidos para saciar la sed. Sabrás que estás tomando suficiente líquido si tu orina es transparente o de color amarillo pálido. Utiliza cada toma como recordatorio para comer un refrigerio ligero o tomar alguna bebida.

Puedes limitar la cantidad de visitantes y la duración de las visitas colocando un pequeño letrero de "No molestar" en la puerta de tu casa.

Puedes comenzar a hacer ejercicio ligero de 2 a 4 semanas después de que nazca el bebé, pero escucha lo que te diga tu cuerpo. Muchas madres, ansiosas por bajar el peso que subieron durante el embarazo, realizan demasiadas actividades en forma prematura y rápidamente se arrepienten. Si tienes alguna pregunta acerca de qué actividades son seguras, habla con tu proveedor de atención para la salud. ¡Recuerda, estas primeras semanas son una experiencia de aprendizaje para toda la familia, así que relájate y disfruta de esta época con ellos!

Algunas madres se sienten cómodas al amamantar
frente a sus familiares y amigos, pero otras no.

¿Cómo puedo comprobar si mi bebé está comiendo suficiente?

Muchas madres se preocupan porque no saben si su bebé está comiendo suficiente. El estómago de tu bebé es del tamaño de su puño, así que es fácil producir suficiente leche para llenarlo. ¡Solo recuerda que nada saldrá por abajo a menos que entre por arriba! Puedes estar segura de que tu bebé está obteniendo suficiente alimento si...

- está activo y alerta.
- queda contento y satisfecho después de amamantarse.
- se amamanta por lo menos ocho veces cada 24 horas.
- chupa y traga mientras se amamanta.
- baja menos del 7 por ciento de su peso al nacer.
- aumenta de 4 a 8 onzas por semana después de la primera semana.
- hace popó tres o más veces al día y moja los pañales seis o más veces al día para el quinto día de nacido.
- hace popó amarilla para el quinto día.
- produce orina transparente o de color amarillo pálido.

Si no estás segura de que tu bebé esté comiendo lo suficiente, continúa dándole el pecho y llama a su proveedor de atención para la salud o a tu clínica WIC (consulta la sección "¿Qué es WIC?" en la página 122).

 Mamás que comparten consejos acerca de cómo saber si el bebé tiene hambre: **babygooroo.com/video/hungry/sp**

 Mamás que comparten consejos acerca de cómo saber si el bebé está comiendo suficiente: **babygooroo.com/video/enough/sp**

¿Qué apariencia debe tener la evacuación (popó) de mi bebé?

La buena noticia es que la popó de los bebés que se amamantan no huele mal. ¡La mala noticia es que hacen mucha!

Podrás saber que tu bebé está comiendo suficiente por el color de la popó y la cantidad de evacuaciones.

La evacuación de tu bebé será...

- negra, espesa y pegajosa durante el primero y segundo días.
- verde y pastosa para el tercer día.
- amarilla, aguada y con apariencia de semillas para el quinto día.

Después del segundo día, el bebé evacuará tres o más veces al día. A medida que crezca tu bebé, la cantidad y el tamaño de las evacuaciones cambiará. Después de 6 semanas, algunos bebés continuarán teniendo tres o más evacuaciones por día. Otros evacuan con menos frecuencia (cada 1 a 5 días), pero producen evacuaciones más grandes.

DÍA	1	2	3	4	5	6	7
CANTIDAD	1+	1+	3+	3+	3+	3+	3+
COLOR	Negra	Negra	Verde	Verde	Amarilla	Amarilla	Amarilla

Cantidad y color de las evacuaciones durante la primera semana.

 Si tu bebé tiene evacuaciones negras al tercer día, evacuaciones verdes al quinto día o menos evacuaciones de las esperadas en cualquier día, llama de inmediato a su proveedor de atención para la salud.

¿Cómo puedo evitar que mi bebé sufra el síndrome de muerte súbita infantil?

El síndrome de muerte súbita infantil es la principal causa de muerte en los bebés de 1 mes a 1 año de edad. El síndrome de muerte súbita infantil ocurre con mayor frecuencia entre los 2 y los 4 meses de edad. Este síndrome se conoce comúnmente como "muerte de cuna" porque la mayoría de los bebés mueren mientras duermen.

La mejor forma de mantener seguro a tu bebé contra el síndrome de muerte súbita infantil es colocarlo siempre de espaldas para dormir. Nunca coloques a tu bebé boca abajo ni de lado para dormir.

La Academia Americana de Pediatría recomienda que las madres duerman cerca de los bebés (en la misma habitación), pero no en la misma cama. Los estudios demuestran que cuando las madres y los bebés duermen en la misma habitación es más fácil alimentarlos durante la noche, ambos pueden dormir más y los bebés tienen menos riesgo de sufrir el síndrome de muerte súbita infantil.

Otras sugerencias para evitar que tu bebé sufra el síndrome de muerte súbita infantil incluyen:

- Amamanta a tu bebé.

- Coloca a tu bebé sobre un colchón firme u otra superficie firme para dormir. Nunca acuestes a tu bebé para dormir sobre una cama de agua, un sofá o una silla.

- Viste al bebé con una sola capa de ropa. No dejes que le dé demasiado calor.

- Coloca a tu bebé en un saco para dormir. Incluso las cobijas o cobertores ligeros pueden atrapar a tu bebé.

- No coloques almohadas, ropa de cama pesada o suelta, ni juguetes rellenos en la cama de tu bebé.

- Mantén a tu bebé en un ambiente donde no haya humo de cigarrillos. No fumes durante el embarazo ni durante el primer año de vida de tu bebé.

- Lleva a tu bebé a las visitas regulares de control y a las vacunaciones.

- Llama de inmediato al proveedor de atención para la salud de tu bebé si este parece estar enfermo.

Amamanta a tu bebé y colócalo de espaldas para dormir para ayudar a impedir que sufra el síndrome de muerte súbita infantil.

¿Puedo dormir con mi bebé?

Con frecuencia los bebés duermen en varios lugares, como en el asiento del auto, en la cuna, en una cama con barandales, en el moisés, en una cuna lateral (del tipo que se coloca al lado de la cama de los adultos) y en la cama de los adultos. Aunque algunos lugares para dormir son seguros, otros pueden aumentar el riesgo del síndrome de muerte súbita infantil para el bebé. Ciertas afecciones o conductas también pueden hacer que los lugares seguros se vuelvan inseguros.

La Academia Americana de Pediatría (American Academy of Pediatrics, AAP) recomienda que las madres duerman cerca de los bebés (en la misma habitación), pero no en la misma cama. Los estudios demuestran que cuando las madres y los bebés duermen en la misma habitación es más fácil alimentarlos durante la noche, ambos pueden dormir más y los bebés tienen menos riesgo de sufrir el síndrome de muerte súbita infantil.

Aunque los médicos recomiendan que las madres y los bebés duerman en camas separadas, muchas madres duermen con sus bebés durante parte de la noche o toda la noche, en forma ocasional o permanente. Si decides dormir con tu bebé en la misma cama, las siguientes sugerencias te ayudarán a mantenerlo seguro y a evitar el síndrome de muerte súbita infantil.

- Coloca siempre al bebé sobre la espalda para dormir. No coloques nunca al bebé boca abajo o de lado.
- No duermas con tu bebé en una cama de agua, un sofá o una silla.
- No coloques a tu bebé solo en una cama para adultos.
- No coloques a tu bebé en una cama para adultos con otros niños.
- Los padres que están demasiado cansados no deben dormir con sus bebés.
- Los padres que fuman no deben dormir con sus bebés.
- Los padres no deben dormir con sus bebés si han consumido alcohol o drogas.
- Los padres que tienen sobrepeso (obesidad) no deben dormir con sus bebés.

Si tienes alguna pregunta acerca de si puedes dormir con tu bebé, habla con tu proveedor de atención para la salud.

La Academia Americana de Pediatría recomienda que las madres duerman cerca de los bebés, pero en camas separadas.

¿Cuándo dormirá mi bebé toda la noche?

Después de que tu bebé comience a tomar bien el pecho y a subir de peso, puedes comenzar a permitirle que establezca su propio horario de alimentación. Esto puede suceder de 4 a 6 semanas después de nacer. Recuerda que cada bebé es diferente. Algunos bebés se amamantan cada 2 a 3 horas, de día y de noche, durante muchas semanas. Otros se amamantan cada hora o cada 2 horas cuando están despiertos, y duermen durante períodos más largos. Para cuando cumplen entre 6 y 12 semanas de edad, muchos bebés duermen desde la medianoche hasta las 4 o 5 de la mañana. ¡Simplemente, lo que tienes que hacer es cambiar tus ideas acerca de lo que es la noche!

¿Cómo puedo evitar que se le aplane la cabeza a mi bebé?

El cerebro de tu bebé necesita espacio para crecer, así que la cabeza está formada por huesos suaves que se unen con el tiempo. Cuando los bebés pasan mucho tiempo en una sola posición, es posible que se les forme una zona plana en la cabeza y que el cabello les crezca muy poco ahí. Esto se conoce como plagiocefalia. La plagiocefalia es una palabra elegante que significa cabeza plana.

Los bebés prematuros tienen más probabilidades de desarrollar una zona plana en la cabeza, debido a que esta es aún más suave que la de los bebés que nacen a término. Los bebés prematuros con frecuencia pasan más tiempo acostados de espaldas sin que nadie los mueva o los cargue. Para evitar que se les aplane la cabeza, a los padres de los bebés prematuros se les invita a que carguen a sus bebés colocados piel con piel contra el pecho. Esto se conoce como cuidado de canguro (incluso los bebés a término se benefician con el cuidado de canguro).

Los bebés que duermen de espaldas tienen menos riesgo de sufrir el síndrome de muerte súbita infantil, así que siempre debes colocar a tu bebé de espaldas para dormir. Puedes evitar que a tu bebé se le aplane la cabeza colocándolo boca abajo cuando esté despierto o cargándolo en posición vertical en una canguera. El tiempo que pase sobre el estómago también

le fortalecerá los músculos necesarios para gatear y sentarse.
Como el riesgo de sufrir el síndrome de muerte súbita infantil
es mayor cuando el bebé se encuentra sobre el estómago, no
lo dejes solo durante el tiempo que pase en esa posición. Si
necesitas dejar solo a tu bebé, aunque sea por un minuto o
dos, acuéstalo de espaldas. Puedes volver a colocarlo sobre el
estómago cuando regreses.

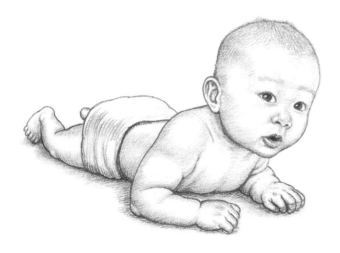

Colocar a los bebés sobre el estómago mientras están despiertos
fortalece los músculos necesarios para gatear y sentarse,
y ayuda a evitar que se les aplane la cabeza.

Como el riesgo de sufrir el síndrome de muerte súbita infantil es mayor cuando el bebé se encuentra sobre el estómago, no lo dejes solo durante el tiempo que pase en esa posición.

¿Cómo puedo tranquilizar al bebé cuando llora?

Los bebés lloran por muchas razones, y algunos lloran más que otros. A veces es fácil descubrir la causa del llanto, pero con frecuencia no es posible hacerlo. Muchos bebés pasan por períodos de inquietud al final de la tarde o durante las primeras horas de la noche. Algunos bebés dejan de llorar al cargarlos, acurrucarlos, mecerlos o bañarlos. Se requiere tiempo para descubrir cómo calmar a tu bebé, así que ten paciencia.

La mejor forma de detener el llanto es revisar cada una de las causas posibles. Es posible que el pañal de tu bebé esté mojado o sucio. O quizás tenga hambre, esté cansado, tenga frío o calor, o esté aburrido. Pronto descubrirás qué formas de consuelo funcionan mejor. Si el llanto persiste, es posible que tu bebé esté enfermo. Tómale la temperatura y llama a su proveedor de atención para la salud si tiene fiebre.

Es posible que haya ocasiones en que no puedas sobrellevar el llanto de tu bebé. Si esto sucede, dáselo a alguien más para que lo cuide o colócalo en un lugar seguro como una cuna o un corralito y tómate un descanso. Haz algo que te relaje, como escuchar música o tomar un baño.

¿Puedo darle chupón a mi bebé?

Mientras más seguido amamantes a tu bebé, más pronto aprenderán ambos esta importante destreza. Si utilizas un chupón en las primeras semanas, es posible que tu bebé se amamante con menos frecuencia y quizás no aprenda a hacerlo bien. Algunos estudios sugieren que el uso del chupón mientras el bebé duerme puede reducir el riesgo del síndrome de muerte súbita infantil. Sin embargo, lo mejor es esperar hasta que tu bebé se amamante bien (aproximadamente de 4 a 6 semanas después de nacer) antes de ofrecerle un chupón. ¡Muchos bebés que se amamantan prefieren chuparse los pulgares, los dedos o los puños!

¿Necesito darle vitaminas a mi bebé?

Tu bebé necesita una sola dosis de vitamina K y una dosis diaria de vitamina D. El proveedor de atención médica de tu bebé le dará la vitamina K poco después de nacer. La principal fuente de vitamina D de tu bebé es la luz solar. Debido a que la cantidad de luz solar que recibe tu bebé es difícil de medir, y como el exceso de esta puede ser dañino, muchos proveedores de atención para la salud recomiendan que los bebés reciban una dosis de 400 UI de vitamina D todos los días desde poco después de nacer. Puedes adquirir la vitamina en gotas, que se venden sin receta. Sigue cuidadosamente las instrucciones del paquete para asegurarte de que tu bebé reciba la cantidad correcta de vitamina D cada día.

Durante las últimas semanas del embarazo, los bebés almacenan suficiente hierro en el hígado para satisfacer sus necesidades de hierro durante aproximadamente 6 meses. Después de 6 meses, los bebés reciben el hierro que necesitan de los alimentos ricos en este mineral, como la carne y el cereal fortificado con hierro. El proveedor de atención para la salud de tu bebé te informará si necesita hierro más pronto, y es posible que te recomiende un suplemento de este mineral.

¿Cuánto tiempo debe amamantarse mi bebé?

Algunas madres dan lactancia durante algunas semanas, otras durante algunos meses y otras más durante algunos años. Cualquier cantidad de lactancia que des es buena para ti y para tu bebé. La cantidad de tiempo que amamantes a tu bebé dependerá de tus necesidades y de las de tu hijo.

Algunos bebés comienzan a perder interés en la lactancia entre los 6 y los 12 meses, cuando se les ofrecen alimentos sólidos. Sin embargo, la leche materna debe continuar siendo una parte importante de la alimentación de tu bebé. El reemplazo de la leche materna por otros alimentos se conoce como destete. Lo que es más importante que el momento en que se realiza el destete es hacerlo lentamente. Algunos bebés se destetan por completo entre los 12 y los 24 meses de edad. Otros continúan amamantándose esporádicamente durante 3 o 4 años o más, ya que el seno es un lugar maravilloso para comer, dormir y acurrucarse.

Consejos para un destete lento

- Reemplaza una toma de leche a la vez con sólidos o líquidos, dependiendo de la edad y destreza de tu bebé. Quizás desees pedirle a otro miembro de tu familia, como el padre, el hermano o la hermana del bebé, que le ofrezca el alimento sustituto. Reemplaza una de las tomas diarias cada 3 a 5 días hasta completar el destete.

- Aumenta el tiempo que dedicas a acurrucar al bebé. Tu bebé puede seguir encontrando bienestar y seguridad en tus brazos.

- Mantén ocupado al niño pequeño con juegos, actividades al aire libre y narración de cuentos.

- Es de esperar que continúes produciendo leche durante muchos días, o incluso muchas semanas, después de que el destete haya terminado.

A veces sucede algo (accidente o enfermedad) que hace necesario que la mamá destete rápidamente al bebé.

Consejos para un destete rápido

- Extrae o bombea una cantidad pequeña de leche para aliviar el llenado y evitar la inflamación. Extrae solamente la leche suficiente para aliviar el llenado. Mientras más leche te extraigas, más leche producirás.

- Colócate paquetes fríos sobre los senos para aliviar el dolor y reducir la inflamación.

- Utiliza un sostén ajustado que sea cómodo y te dé soporte.

- Toma acetaminofeno (Tylenol) o ibuprofeno (Advil) para el dolor. Tu proveedor de atención para la salud puede sugerirte otros medicamentos para el dolor si es necesario.

Algunos niños continúan amamantándose en forma
esporádica durante 3, 4 o más años.

¿Cuándo debo darle alimento sólido a mi bebé?

Del nacimiento a los 6 meses

La leche materna es el único alimento que tu bebé necesita durante aproximadamente los primeros 6 meses de vida. Si comienzas a darle alimentos sólidos demasiado pronto, puedes causarle estreñimiento, diarrea, gases, vómitos o alergias.

Sabrás que tu bebé está listo para tomar alimentos sólidos cuando se pueda sentar, voltear la cabeza, ponerse alimentos en la boca y tragar.

De los 6 meses al año de edad

Cuando tu bebé tenga aproximadamente 6 meses de edad, podrás comenzar a ofrecerle alimentos sólidos. Sabrás que tu bebé está listo para tomar alimentos sólidos si se puede sentar, voltear la cabeza, ponerse alimentos en la boca y tragar. Aunque los alimentos sólidos le proporcionan vitaminas y nutrientes, la leche materna debe ser una parte fundamental de la alimentación de tu bebé durante por lo menos un año.

Si dejas de darle lactancia a tu bebé antes de que tenga un año de edad, pídele a su proveedor de atención para la salud que te recomiende una fórmula rica en hierro. Tu bebé debe tener por lo menos un año de edad antes de que comiences a darle leche de vaca.

Mamás y papás que comparten consejos acerca de cómo saber si tu bebé está listo para comer alimentos sólidos:
babygooroo.com/video/solids/sp

Tu leche es el único alimento que tu bebé necesita durante aproximadamente los primeros 6 meses.

¿Qué son los períodos de crecimiento acelerado?

Puede haber muchas ocasiones en que tu bebé crezca más rápido que lo usual. Estos se conocen como períodos de crecimiento acelerado. Un aumento súbito en la cantidad de veces que el bebé se amamanta puede ser una señal de un período de crecimiento acelerado. Los períodos de crecimiento acelerado con frecuencia ocurren alrededor de las 3 semanas, las 6 semanas, los 3 meses y los 6 meses de edad. Sin embargo, los períodos de crecimiento acelerado pueden ocurrir en cualquier momento. Debido a que tu bebé desea comer todo el tiempo, es posible que tus familiares y amigos te digan que "no estás produciendo suficiente leche", que "necesitas darle alimentos sólidos o fórmula a tu bebé" o que "ya es hora de dejar de darle el pecho". Ten paciencia. Después de 2 a 3 días, tu suministro de leche aumentará y tu bebé te pedirá el pecho con menos frecuencia.

¿Qué son las huelgas de lactancia?

Una huelga de lactancia es cuando el bebé de pronto se rehúsa a amamantar. A veces la huelga tiene una causa clara, como cuando al bebé le salen los dientes, tiene fiebre, una infección en el oído, la nariz tapada (resfriado), está estreñido o tiene diarrea. El desodorante, el perfume o el talco en la piel de la madre también pueden provocar una huelga. A veces no es posible encontrar la causa. Será necesario que te extraigas la leche a mano o con un sacaleche hasta que la huelga termine. Mientras tanto, dale a tu bebé la leche que te extraigas utilizando una cucharita, un gotero, una cuchara para medicina con el mango hueco o una taza. Vigila a tu bebé para detectar las primeras señales de hambre y ofrécele el seno en ese momento. Amamanta a tu bebé en un lugar tranquilo. Dale toda tu atención a tu bebé. Las huelgas de lactancia casi nunca llevan al destete.

CAPÍTULO 5
CÓMO AMAMANTAR A BEBÉS ESPECIALES

¿Puedo amamantar si tengo más de un bebé?

Muchas madres producen suficiente leche para satisfacer las necesidades de dos (o más) bebés. Mientras más leche tomen tus bebés de tus senos, más leche producirás.

Al principio, quizás sea más fácil que alimentes a un bebé a la vez. Sin embargo, después de que tú y tus bebés aprendan a amamantar bien, podrás ahorrar tiempo al alimentarlos a ambos a la vez. Algunos bebés se amamantan solo en un seno durante cada toma, mientras que otros se amamantan en ambos. Solamente recuerda que cada bebé necesita amamantarse por lo menos ocho veces cada 24 horas.

Dos o más bebés requieren más tiempo, sin importar cómo decidas alimentarlos. Así que no olvides cuidarte a ti misma y a tus bebés. Consume diversos alimentos saludables, toma suficientes líquidos para satisfacer la sed y acepta los ofrecimientos de ayuda de tus familiares y amigos.

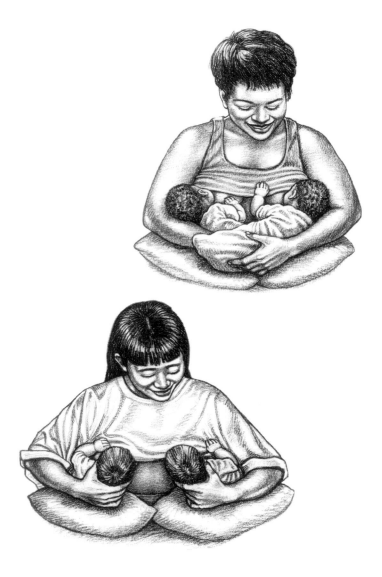

Amamantar a dos bebés a la vez ahorra tiempo y energía.

¿Puedo amamantar a mi bebé si nace antes de tiempo?

El nacimiento de un bebé pequeñito que nace semanas o meses antes de tiempo puede ser atemorizante. Es posible que tengas muchas preguntas.

- ¿Por qué sucedió esto?
- ¿Será algo que hice?
- ¿Cómo comerá si es demasiado pequeño para succionar?
- ¿Puedo darle el pecho?

Los bebés que nacen prematuramente, incluso los que necesitan atención especial, pueden amamantarse. La lactancia les da a los padres la oportunidad de participar en la atención de su bebé y de hacer algo que nadie más puede hacer. La leche de las madres que tienen bebés prematuros contiene la cantidad precisa de nutrientes para satisfacer incluso las necesidades de los bebés más prematuros.

Infórmale al personal del hospital que planeas dar lactancia. Aunque tu bebé sea demasiado pequeño o esté demasiado enfermo para amamantarse, es posible alimentarlo con tu leche. El personal del hospital puede mostrarte cómo extraerte la leche y cómo almacenarla.

En cuanto tu bebé esté suficientemente bien como para cargarlo durante un período de tiempo cada día, pregúntale a la enfermera si lo puedes colocar debajo de tu ropa para acurrucarlo piel con piel contra tu pecho (cuidado de canguro).

El proveedor de atención para la salud de tu bebé te dirá cuándo está listo para amamantarse.

Los bebés que se colocan piel con piel respiran de manera más uniforme, suben más rápido de peso, salen más pronto del hospital para ir a casa y tienen más probabilidades de amamantarse.

¿Puedo amamantar si tuve un parto por cesárea?

Las madres que tuvieron una operación cesárea sí pueden amamantar. Si la madre o el bebé necesitan atención especial, se puede retrasar el inicio de la lactancia. Si tuviste un parto por cesárea, quizás encuentres útiles las siguientes sugerencias.

- Elije una posición cómoda. Utiliza almohadas adicionales para proteger la incisión (herida) y apoyarte. Las mejores posiciones son la reclinada de lado o la de balón de fútbol americano.

- Mantén a tu bebé contigo en tu habitación para ahorrar tiempo y energía.

- Descansa mucho. Toma siestas al mismo tiempo que tu bebé.

- Limita tus actividades. Trata de no levantar cosas pesadas, no hagas las tareas del hogar y no realices ejercicios enérgicos durante 4 a 6 semanas.

- Quizás necesites medicamentos para el dolor durante varios días. Tu proveedor de atención para la salud te recomendará medicinas que sean seguras para ti y para tu bebé.

Selecciona una posición cómoda y utiliza almohadas
adicionales para proteger la incisión.

CAPÍTULO 6
CÓMO CUIDARTE A TI MISMA

¿Qué debo hacer si tengo los senos inflamados y duros?

Durante la primera semana después de que nazca tu bebé, tu suministro de leche aumentará en forma constante y es posible que sientas los senos llenos y pesados. La lactancia frecuente ayudará a aliviar el llenado, pero si retrasas u omites la toma, es posible que los senos se inflamen, se endurezcan y te causen dolor.

Sugerencias para aliviar la inflamación de los senos

- Extrae a mano o con un sacaleche una cantidad pequeña de leche o calostro. Esto suavizará el seno y permitirá que el bebé se prenda con más facilidad.

- Utiliza paquetes fríos entre las tomas para reducir la inflamación. Puedes usar bolsas de chícharos (guisantes) congelados envueltas en una toallita mojada y fresca.

- Aumenta el flujo de leche apretando suavemente el seno cuando tu bebé haga pausas durante la alimentación.

- Amamanta cada 1 a 3 horas durante el día y cada 2 a 3 horas durante la noche.

- Utiliza un sostén cómodo que te dé soporte, pero asegúrate de que te quede bien y no esté demasiado ajustado.

Aumenta el flujo de leche apretando suavemente el seno cuando tu bebé haga pausas durante la alimentación.

Después de varias semanas, tu suministro de leche cambiará
para satisfacer las necesidades de tu bebé, y es posible que tus
senos luzcan más pequeños y menos llenos.

No te preocupes si tus senos parecen estar menos
llenos. ¡Esto no quiere decir que estás perdiendo la
leche! Simplemente, tu suministro está cambiando
para satisfacer las necesidades de tu bebé.

¿Qué debo hacer si tengo los pezones adoloridos?

Es posible que sientas los pezones adoloridos durante la primera semana en que tú y tu bebé estén aprendiendo a amamantar. Muchas madres sienten un tirón o un jalón doloroso cuando el bebé se prende al seno. Esto es común. Si tu bebé está bien colocado, el dolor debe durar solo unos segundos. Si sientes dolor durante más de unos segundos, es posible que el bebé no esté bien prendido. Interrumpe la succión, retira al bebé del seno e inténtalo de nuevo.

Sugerencias para aliviar los pezones adoloridos

- Comienza cada toma con el seno que esté menos adolorido. Antes de que tu bebé se prenda, puedes iniciar el flujo de leche colocando una toalla tibia y húmeda sobre el seno o senos adoloridos y dándote un masaje suave.

- Si tienes los senos llenos y duros, extrae una cantidad pequeña de leche o calostro para ablandarlos.

- Coloca correctamente a tu bebé en el seno. Recuerda, la barbilla del bebé debe tocar el seno y la boca debe estar bien abierta.

- Sostén a tu bebé cerca de ti para evitar que te jale los pezones. Recuerda interrumpir la succión antes de desprender al bebé del seno.

- Si es necesario, amamántalo más seguido (cada 1 o 2 horas) y durante períodos más cortos (10 a 15 minutos o hasta que el seno se ablande).

- No es necesario que te laves los pezones antes de cada toma. Incluso el agua limpia, cuando se utiliza con frecuencia, reseca la piel.

- Después de cada lactancia, aplica una cantidad pequeña de leche materna sobre la areola y el pezón de cada seno. Si tienes los pezones resecos y adoloridos, puedes utilizar lanolina modificada en lugar de leche. ¡Con un poco es suficiente!

- Si tienes los pezones adoloridos, agrietados o sangrantes, llama a tu proveedor de atención para la salud.

¿Cómo puedo evitar que me goteen los senos?

El goteo ocurre a veces cuando piensas en tu bebé, si escuchas que él u otro bebé está llorando o si retrasas una toma. ¡Los senos también pueden gotear al tener relaciones sexuales!

Sugerencias para controlar el goteo

- Puedes detener el flujo de leche presionando las palmas de las manos contra los pezones o cruzando los brazos sobre el pecho.

- Utiliza protectores absorbentes para proteger la ropa. Cambia los protectores con frecuencia y no utilices protectores forrados de plástico que atrapen la humedad.

- Para ocultar la humedad, viste ropa de color claro y estampado pequeño.

- Amamanta a tu bebé antes de tener relaciones sexuales.

¿Necesito cambiar lo que como?

¡Puedes comer todo lo que comías antes! Selecciona una amplia variedad de alimentos: verduras, frutas, pan, cereal, arroz, pasta, carne, pescado, aves, frijoles, huevos, yogurt, leche y queso. Toma suficientes líquidos para que no tengas sed. El agua, la leche sin grasa o con bajo contenido de grasa y el jugo de fruta sin endulzar son buenas opciones. Sabrás que estás tomando suficientes líquidos si tu orina es transparente o de color amarillo pálido.

Algunas madres descubren que ciertos alimentos hacen que sus bebés se sientan inquietos. Si esto sucede, simplemente mantente alejada de esos alimentos.

Consume una amplia variedad de alimentos: verduras, frutas, pan, cereal, arroz, pasta, carne, aves, pescado, frijoles, huevos, yogurt, leche y queso.

¿Puedo tomar bebidas alcohólicas?

Las bebidas alcohólicas (cerveza, vino o licor) pasan
fácilmente a la leche materna, e incluso las cantidades
pequeñas pueden afectar tu capacidad de atender a tu bebé.
Si decides tomar bebidas alcohólicas, no tomes más de una
o dos por semana y espera por lo menos 2 horas después de
consumirlas para amamantar a tu bebé.

¿Puedo fumar o masticar tabaco?

El humo del cigarrillo y la nicotina pueden ser dañinos no solo para ti sino también para tu bebé. Los bebés que viven con fumadores (mamás, papás, abuelos, etc.) tienen más probabilidades de sufrir infecciones en los oídos, pulmonía y asma. También tienen más probabilidades de padecer el síndrome de muerte súbita infantil. Mientras más cigarrillos fumen tú o algún habitante de tu casa, mayores serán los riesgos de salud para tu bebé.

Para las madres que están dando lactancia, fumar se ha relacionado con una reducción en la producción de leche y un destete prematuro, aunque se desconoce la causa exacta de esto. Debes amamantar aunque fumes o masques tabaco y no puedas dejar de hacerlo. Es posible que la leche materna contrarreste algunos de los efectos negativos del humo del cigarrillo, así que es mejor fumar menos y dar lactancia que alimentar con fórmula.

Para limitar la exposición de tu bebé a los químicos tóxicos de los cigarrillos, ten a la mano una camiseta extra grande y póntela encima de la ropa cuando fumes. No fumes ni permitas que otros lo hagan en tu casa, en tu auto o cerca de tu bebé.

¿Puedo dar lactancia si consumo drogas ilegales?

Las drogas que se venden en las calles (crack, heroína y mariguana) pueden dañar tu salud y la de tu bebé. Las drogas ilegales se transfieren a tu leche y a tu bebé, y pueden hacer que se le dificulte comer, dormir, respirar y crecer. Las madres que consumen drogas ilegales no deben amamantar.

¿Puedo dar lactancia y al mismo tiempo bajar de peso?

Las madres que amamantan con frecuencia bajan de peso con más facilidad que las madres que no lo hacen. Esto sucede porque algunas de las calorías necesarias para producir la leche materna provienen de la grasa almacenada durante el embarazo. El resto de las calorías proviene de los alimentos que comes. Recuerda comer una amplia variedad de alimentos saludables todos los días (verduras, frutas, panes, cereales, carne, pescado, aves, huevos, leche y queso), así como hacer ejercicio con regularidad.

Para bajar el peso que subiste...

- toma leche sin grasa o con bajo contenido de grasa, agua o jugo de fruta sin endulzar.

- come menos alimentos que contengan azúcar como galletas, dulces, pasteles y helado.

- come refrigerios de frutas frescas y verduras crudas.

- hornea o asa la carne y el pescado.

- haz ejercicio (camina, pasea en bicicleta o corre) todos los días.

¿Qué pasa si me enfermo y necesito medicamentos?

A menos que tengas una enfermedad seria como VIH/SIDA, la mejor protección para tu bebé es tu leche, así que continúa dándole el pecho.

Consulta con tu proveedor de atención para la salud antes de tomar cualquier medicamento, incluidos los de venta libre (sin receta). Asegúrate de que tu proveedor de atención para la salud sepa que estás dando lactancia para que pueda recomendarte medicamentos seguros para ti y para tu bebé.

Cuídate a ti misma y a tu bebé. Mantén a tu bebé contigo en tu habitación y duerme al mismo tiempo que él. Pídeles a tus familiares y amigos que te ayuden con las tareas del hogar.

Si tienes que permanecer en el hospital, infórmale al personal que estás dando lactancia y pregúntales si tu bebé puede quedarse contigo.

Si necesitas alejarte de tu bebé, puedes extraerte la leche de los senos a mano o con un sacaleche para aliviar el llenado y mantener tu suministro de leche. Es posible que el hospital o la clínica de WIC tengan un sacaleche que puedas usar (consulta la sección "Qué es WIC" en la página 122). La mayoría de los bebés vuelven a amamantarse si se les da la oportunidad. Si tu bebé rehúsa amamantarse, pídele ayuda a tu proveedor de atención para la salud.

¿Qué es la "tristeza posparto" y en qué se diferencia de la "depresión posparto"?

Después de que nazca tu bebé, es posible que te sientas contenta durante un minuto y triste al siguiente. Incluso, es posible que llores sin razón aparente. Estos son síntomas de la "tristeza posparto". Muchas madres experimentan la tristeza posparto. Los síntomas son normales, usualmente ocurren de 3 a 4 días después del parto y duran varios días.

Si tus síntomas duran más tiempo o empeoran, es posible que tengas una enfermedad más seria conocida como "depresión posparto". La depresión posparto puede ocurrir inmediatamente después del nacimiento, o semanas o meses después. La depresión posparto es una enfermedad, no una debilidad. Los síntomas de la depresión posparto incluyen:

- no querer cuidarte a ti misma o a tu bebé
- pérdida de apetito
- falta de energía
- problemas para dormir
- sentimiento de tristeza o culpabilidad
- sentir ansiedad o sentirte asustada
- sentirte enojada
- pensar en hacerte daño a ti misma o a tu bebé

Nadie sabe qué es lo que causa la depresión posparto, pero es posible que tenga que ver con los cambios hormonales que ocurren durante el embarazo y después del parto. Estos cambios hormonales pueden causar cambios químicos en el cerebro y llevar a la depresión.

La depresión posparto puede durar varias semanas o muchos meses. Sin embargo, es importante saber que la depresión posparto no dura para siempre. Mientras más rápido obtengas ayuda, más pronto comenzarás a sentirte mejor.

Estas son algunas ideas que otras madres que han tenido depresión posparto han encontrado útiles:

- Está bien que te sientas abrumada. El parto suscita muchos cambios y la crianza de los hijos no es fácil.

- Busca a alguien con quién hablar y cuéntale cómo te sientes.

- Sé honesta acerca de lo que puedes y no puedes hacer, y pídele ayuda a los demás.

- Busca a alguien que te ayude con el cuidado de los hijos y las tareas del hogar.

- Haz algo por ti cada día, aunque sea durante solamente 15 minutos. Algunas opciones son leer, hacer ejercicio (caminar es bueno para ti y es fácil hacerlo), tomar un baño o escuchar música.

- Acepta el hecho de que algunos días solo podrás hacer una cosa. Quizás haya días en que no puedas hacer nada. Trata de no enojarte cuando esto suceda.

- Escribe lo que piensas y lo que sientes todos los días. Una vez que comiences a sentirte mejor, leer de nuevo lo que escribiste te ayudará a darte cuenta de que estás mejorando.

- Habla con tu proveedor de atención para la salud acerca de tus sentimientos. Tu proveedor puede ofrecerte consejos o medicamentos que sean seguros para ti y para tu bebé.

¿Y el sexo?

Es posible que al principio tengas poco interés en el sexo. Tener un nuevo bebé requiere tiempo y energía. A muchas mujeres les preocupa que el sexo les resulte doloroso o que puedan quedar embarazadas de nuevo. Dile a tu compañero cómo te sientes.

Antes de tener relaciones sexuales, habla con tu proveedor de atención para la salud acerca de los métodos anticonceptivos y selecciona uno que se adapte a tu estilo de vida.

Cuando tengas relaciones sexuales, es posible que te gotee leche de los senos. Puedes ayudar a evitar esto si amamantas a tu bebé antes de hacer el amor. Esto te dará más tiempo para tener relaciones sexuales o dormir, ¡lo que suceda primero!

Mientras estés amamantando, es posible que se te reseque la vagina y que el sexo te resulte incómodo. Puede ser útil usar un lubricante como la jalea K-Y. Aplica una cantidad pequeña alrededor de la abertura de la vagina antes de tener relaciones sexuales.

¿Puedo tomar píldoras anticonceptivas mientras estoy amamantando?

La mayoría de las mujeres desean planear sus embarazos. Si esperas por lo menos un año antes de embarazarte de nuevo, tu cuerpo tendrá oportunidad de recuperarse.

Las píldoras anticonceptivas que contienen estrógenos pueden reducir tu suministro de leche, pero se piensa que las píldoras anticonceptivas que solo contienen progesterona son seguras. Algunas madres observan una reducción en su suministro de leche incluso cuando toman píldoras que solo contienen progesterona, así que es mejor esperar hasta que tengas un buen suministro de leche (por lo menos 6 semanas después de que nazca tu bebé) antes de tomar píldoras que contengan progesterona.

Si tu suministro de leche se reduce, habla con tu proveedor de atención para la salud acerca de otros tipos de anticonceptivos. Existen muchas opciones, entre ellas la planeación natural de la familia, el diafragma, la esponja, el anillo vaginal, el dispositivo intrauterino (DIU), los condones y las cremas, espumas o jaleas espermicidas.

¿Puedo quedar embarazada si estoy amamantando?

Si amamantas en forma exclusiva y nunca o casi nunca le das fórmula, agua u otros alimentos a tu bebé, tendrás menos probabilidades de quedar embarazada. Pero si le das fórmula, agua u otros alimentos a tu bebé, o si el bebé utiliza un chupón con frecuencia, tendrás más probabilidades de quedar embarazada. Si no deseas tener otro bebé pronto, habla con tu proveedor de atención para la salud acerca de los métodos anticonceptivos.

¿Puedo continuar amamantando si me embarazo?

Muchas madres continúan dando el pecho a los bebés más grandes mientras están embarazadas, y algunos de ellos continúan amamantándose después de que nace el nuevo bebé. Esto se conoce como "lactancia en tándem". Para satisfacer las necesidades nutricionales de dos bebés, así como tus propias necesidades, consume gran variedad de alimentos saludables y líquidos para satisfacer la sed, y duerme cuando duerman tus bebés.

CAPÍTULO 7

AL REGRESAR AL TRABAJO O A LA ESCUELA

¿Puedo amamantar después de volver al trabajo o a la escuela?

Muchas madres continúan amamantando después de volver al trabajo o a la escuela. ¡Se requiere un poco de planeación adicional, pero los beneficios valen la pena!

- La lactancia te mantiene cerca de tu bebé aunque se encuentren separados.
- Los bebés que se amamantan son más saludables, incluso los que van a guarderías.
- Los padres que dan lactancia faltan menos al trabajo y pierden menos ingresos.
- La lactancia ahorra tiempo, ya que no es necesario mezclar, medir ni calentar la fórmula.
- La lactancia facilita la vida de los padres, especialmente la de las madres que regresan al trabajo o la escuela.

Aprende a extraer y recolectar tu leche

Si planeas alimentar a tu bebé con tu leche mientras estén separados, será necesario que aprendas a extraerla y recolectarla. Practica desde el principio y con frecuencia para que aprendas esta importante destreza antes de volver al trabajo o a la escuela.

Decide quién cuidará a tu bebé.

Selecciona a un proveedor de atención infantil que...

Si planeas alimentar a tu bebé con tu leche mientras estén separados,
será necesario que aprendas a extraerla y recolectarla.

- proporcione un lugar seguro y limpio para tu bebé.
- entienda y apoye la lactancia.
- haya cuidado antes a bebés que se estén amamantando o esté dispuesto a aprender.
- se encuentre cerca de tu trabajo o escuela si deseas amamantar durante el día.

Comienza a alimentarlo con biberón o taza

Si vas a estar alejada de tu bebé durante el horario de alimentación, necesitas saber que aceptará el alimento en algo que no sea el seno y de alguien que no seas tú. Aproximadamente 2 semanas antes de volver al trabajo, ofrécele tu leche a tu bebé en un biberón o en una taza (los bebés pueden aprender a alimentarse con taza a cualquier edad).

Si utilizas un biberón, prueba diferentes tipos de tetinas o mamilas hasta que encuentres una que tu bebé acepte. Quizás sea más fácil si otra persona le ofrece la leche que te extraigas.

La lactancia ahorra tiempo, ya que no es necesario mezclar, medir ni calentar la fórmula.

Los padres que dan lactancia faltan menos al trabajo y pierden menos ingresos.

¿Cómo me extraigo la leche?

Puedes extraerte la leche a mano o con un sacaleche. Si vas
a necesitar extraer la leche con frecuencia o durante muchas
semanas o meses, puedes rentar o comprar una bomba
eléctrica con un aditamento especial que te permita extraer la
leche de ambos senos a la vez.

Al principio, es posible que obtengas tan poca leche que
solo puedas cubrir el fondo del recipiente recolector. ¡No te
preocupes! Es posible que tardes varios días antes de ver un
aumento en la cantidad de leche extraída. Trata de relajarte y
pensar en tu bebé.

Consejos para extraerte la leche con un sacaleche

Puedes extraerte leche de un seno mientras tu bebé se
amamanta del otro, o puedes extraerte leche entre tomas.
Cuando tu bebé se amamanta, ocurre un reflejo de chorro
de leche. Con frecuencia, las madres que se extraen la leche
mientras dan lactancia obtienen más leche. Si tu bebé no
puede mantener el ritmo del flujo adicional de leche se
separará del seno durante varios segundos hasta que el flujo
disminuya. ¡Quizás desees tener a la mano un paño para
absorber los chorros!

• Antes de comenzar, lávate las manos con agua y jabón, y
  enjuágatelas bien.

• Sigue las instrucciones de tu sacaleche.

Puedes rentar o comprar una bomba eléctrica con un aditamento especial que te permita extraer la leche de ambos senos al mismo tiempo.

- Extrae leche durante 5 a 10 minutos o hasta que el flujo disminuya. Descansa durante 3 a 5 minutos, y después repite el procedimiento una o dos veces.

- Extrae la leche de cada seno hasta que el flujo de leche disminuya y el seno se ablande.

- Lava las piezas de la bomba sacaleche con agua caliente y jabón después de cada uso, y enjuágalas bien.

- Si estás en el trabajo o en la escuela, enjuaga las piezas de la bomba en agua caliente. Cuando llegues a casa, lávalas en agua caliente con jabón.

Con frecuencia, las madres que se extraen la leche
mientras dan lactancia obtienen más leche.

Consejos para extraerte la leche a mano

- Presiónate el seno contra el pecho y después exprímelo suavemente entre el pulgar y los dedos.

- Mueve el pulgar y los dedos alrededor del seno hasta que todas las partes del mismo estén blandas y el flujo de leche disminuya.

Consejos para facilitar la extracción

- Busca un lugar tranquilo y confortable.
- Colócate paños húmedos y tibios sobre los senos.
- Dales masaje a los senos con un movimiento circular.
- Relájate y piensa en tu bebé.

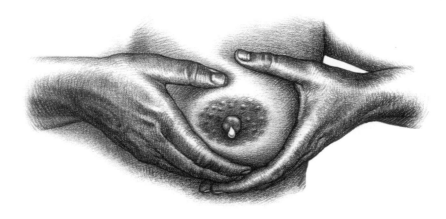

Presiónate el seno contra el pecho y después exprímelo suavemente entre el pulgar y los dedos.

- Escucha música relajante o sonidos tranquilizadores.
- Observa una fotografía de tu bebé.
- Come un refrigerio saludable.

Puedes almacenar tu leche en cualquier recipiente para alimentos. Utiliza algo que no se rompa, se abra o se voltee fácilmente en el refrigerador o congelador. Incluso hay bolsas de plástico especiales para almacenar la leche materna. Coloca el recipiente de leche en un refrigerador o congelador, o guárdalo en un termo o en una hielera.

Un sostén especial que permite que la mamá
se extraiga la leche sin utilizar las manos.

¿Cómo selecciono una bomba sacaleche?

Hay muchos tipos de bombas sacaleche disponibles:

- bombas manuales
- bombas que funcionan con baterías
- bombas eléctricas semiautomáticas
- bombas eléctricas automáticas (ciclo automático)

Ya sea que planees extraerte la leche dos o tres veces al día o dos o tres veces por semana, debes seleccionar una bomba sacaleche que sea cómoda y fácil de usar. La bomba debe ejercer una compresión suave en el seno y extraer la leche con la menor cantidad posible de vacío. ¡La extracción de la leche debe ser rápida, fácil y sin dolor! Algunas características importantes incluyen vacío ajustable, protección contra el flujo de retorno y doble capacidad de bombeo. Las bombas más caras están disponibles para su venta o renta.

Quizás desees esperar hasta después de que nazca tu bebé para comprar o rentar una bomba sacaleche, en caso de que cambien los planes que hiciste durante el embarazo. Estas son algunas cosas que puedes considerar al seleccionar una bomba sacaleche...

- ¿Por qué necesitas una bomba sacaleche?
- ¿Con cuánta frecuencia planeas extraer la leche?
- ¿Es cómoda la bomba?

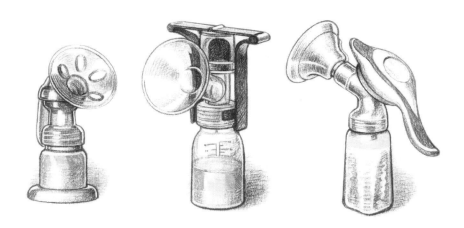

Las bombas manuales están diseñadas para madres que necesitan extraerse leche en forma ocasional.

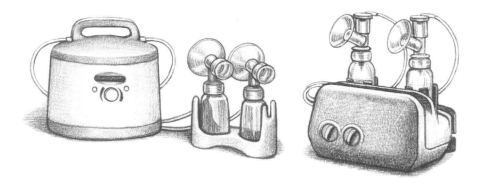

Las bombas completamente automáticas que te permiten extraer leche de ambos senos a la vez están diseñadas para madres que necesitan hacerlo todos los días.

- ¿Es fácil usar la bomba?
- ¿Es fácil limpiar la bomba?
- ¿Cuánto cuesta la bomba?

¿Cuánto tiempo puedo almacenar mi leche?

Maneja tu leche de la misma forma que otros alimentos. Almacena la leche en un lugar fresco, refrigérala en cuanto sea posible y congélala para usarla después. Si vas a almacenar leche para un bebé saludable que nació a término, sigue estas sencillas instrucciones.

- Almacena tu leche en cualquier recipiente para alimentos. Etiqueta el recipiente con tu nombre, el nombre de tu bebé, la fecha y la hora. Coloca una sola porción en cada recipiente.

- Los estudios demuestran que la leche recolectada en condiciones ideales (en recipientes limpios y en temperatura fresca) puede almacenarse hasta 8 horas en una habitación fresca, 8 días en el refrigerador, 8 meses en la sección del congelador de un refrigerador con congelador o 1 año en un congelador vertical u horizontal.

- Muchas veces, sin embargo, es posible que las condiciones no sean ideales. Por seguridad, almacena tu leche en una habitación fresca durante un máximo de 5 horas, en el refrigerador hasta por 5 días, en la sección del congelador de un refrigerador con congelador hasta por 5 meses o un máximo de 1 año en un congelador vertical u horizontal.

- Si se te olvidan estos períodos de almacenamiento, simplemente cuenta los dedos de una mano como recordatorio: ¡cinco!

- Para descongelar la leche, coloca al recipiente sin abrir en el refrigerador o en una olla con agua tibia. No descongeles ni calientes la leche de tu bebé en el horno de microondas, ya que estos destruyen las células vivas y calientan la leche en forma irregular. La leche caliente puede quemar a tu bebé.

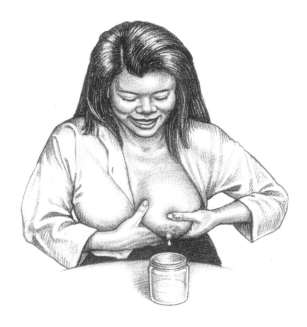

Almacena tu leche en cualquier recipiente limpio para alimentos.

A temperatura ambiente
Hasta 5 horas
a 77 °F o 25 °C

En el congelador
Hasta 5 meses
a 23 °F o -5 °C

En el refrigerador
Hasta 5 días
a 39 °F o 4 °C

En el congelador vertical u horizontal
Hasta 12 meses
a -4 °F o -20 °C

Directrices para el almacenamiento de la leche materna
para bebés saludables nacidos a término

- La leche que descongeles en el refrigerador se debe utilizar en un máximo de 24 horas. La leche descongelada en una olla con agua tibia debe utilizarse de inmediato o guardarse en el refrigerador durante un máximo de 4 horas. La leche que quede en el recipiente de alimentación (es decir, en el biberón o la taza) se puede refrigerar y utilizar para terminar la alimentación.

- La leche materna es fácil de preparar. No requiere calentamiento. Simplemente saca la leche del refrigerador y sírvela. Si tu bebé prefiere la leche a temperatura ambiente, coloca el recipiente sin abrir en una olla con agua tibia durante algunos minutos.

LECHE MATERNA	TEMPERATURA AMBIENTE 77 °F o 25 °C	REFRIGERADOR 39 °F o 4 °C	SECCIÓN DEL CONGELADOR 23 °F o -5 °C	CONGELADOR VERTICAL U HORIZONTAL -4 °F o -20 °C
Fresca	Utilízala en menos de 5 horas	Utilízala en menos de 5 días	Utilízala en menos de 5 meses	Utilízala en menos de 12 meses
Previamente congelada, y después descongelada en el refrigerador	Utilízala en menos de 4 horas	Utilízala en menos de 24 horas	No la congeles de nuevo	No la congeles de nuevo
Previamente congelada, y después descongelada en agua tibia	Utilízala de inmediato	Utilízala en menos de 4 horas	No la congeles de nuevo	No la congeles de nuevo

Directrices para utilizar la leche materna almacenada.

CAPÍTULO 8
CÓMO OBTENER AYUDA

¿Dónde puedo encontrar ayuda para la lactancia?

Existen muchos profesionales de la salud a quienes puedes acudir para obtener ayuda, entre ellos los nutricionistas de WIC, las consultoras en lactancia certificadas por el Consejo Internacional, las líderes de la Liga de la Leche y las compañeras consejeras en lactancia. Tus familiares y amigas que han dado lactancia también pueden ser una fuente de esa motivación y apoyo que es tan necesaria. Si tú o tu bebé tienen un problema médico, comunícate con tu proveedor de atención para la salud o con el del bebé de inmediato.

 Mamás que comparten consejos acerca de dónde encontrar ayud:
babygooroo.com/video/help/sp

Tus familiares y amigas que han dado lactancia pueden ser
una fuente de esa motivación y apoyo que es tan necesaria.

¿Qué es WIC?

WIC (el Programa Especial de Nutrición Complementaria para Mujeres, Bebés y Niños) es un programa especial del gobierno que ofrece alimentos saludables y asesoría de nutrición a las mujeres de pocos recursos que están embarazadas, que recientemente dieron a luz o que están dando lactancia, así como a los niños de hasta 5 años de edad. Casi el 50 por ciento de los bebés que nacen en los Estados Unidos participan en WIC. Los nutricionistas, el personal de enfermería y las compañeras consejeras de WIC ofrecen servicios a entre 7 y 8 millones de mujeres y niños cada mes.

¿Cómo califico para WIC?

Tus ingresos deben estar por debajo de cierto nivel, debes vivir en un área que tenga una clínica de WIC y debes tener un "riesgo nutricional". Un profesional de la salud es quien determina si las mujeres o los niños se encuentran en riesgo nutricional.

Si tus ingresos te permiten participar en programas como el Programa de Ayuda para la Nutrición Complementaria (Supplemental Nutrition Assistance Program, SNAP), Medicaid o la Ayuda Temporal para Familias Necesitadas (Temporary Assistance to Needy Families, TANF), entonces es posible que llenes los requisitos para WIC. También debes cumplir el requisito de residencia y tener un riesgo nutricional para calificar para WIC.

¿Qué alimentos proporciona WIC?

Los paquetes de WIC ahora incluyen alimentos como tortillas, arroz integral, avena, bebidas a base de soya, salmón enlatado, lentejas y tofu, que resultan atractivos para las familias de diversas culturas.

Para garantizar que las mamás y los bebés de WIC tengan una dieta saludable, con bajo contenido de grasa y azúcar y alto contenido de fibra, WIC también ofrece frutas y verduras frescas y congeladas, huevos, leche, queso, pan y cereal integral, mantequilla de cacahuate (maní), frijoles, chícharos (guisantes), leche infantil y alimentos para bebés de frutas, verduras, carnes y cereales.

WIC apoya la lactancia al ofrecerles más alimentos a las madres que amamantan, que incluyen más frutas y verduras, así como carnes y más variedad de frutas y verduras para los bebés que amamantan.

¿Cómo ayuda WIC a las madres que amamantan?

WIC ayuda a las madres que dan lactancia y a sus bebés de muchas maneras.

- Las madres que amamantan a sus bebés pueden participar en WIC hasta que estos cumplen 1 año de edad. Las madres que alimentan con fórmula a sus bebés pueden participar en WIC hasta que estos cumplen 6 meses de edad.

- Las mujeres que dan lactancia reciben más alimentos para ellas y para sus familias.

- Como se sabe que la lactancia es la mejor opción para los bebés, el personal de WIC motiva y apoya esta práctica.

- Algunas clínicas de WIC cuentan con consultoras de lactancia y compañeras consejeras que ofrecen apoyo para la lactancia durante y después del embarazo.

- Algunas clínicas de WIC ofrecen bombas sacaleche para que las madres puedan continuar dando lactancia después de regresar al trabajo o a la escuela.

Para encontrar una clínica de WIC en tu área, consulta con tu departamento de salud local o comunícate con...

USDA Food and Nutrition Service

WIC

Tel: (703) 305-2746

Sitio web: fns.usda.gov/wic/sp-default.htm

Las mujeres que dan lactancia reciben más alimentos para ellas y para sus familias.

¿Qué es una consultora en lactancia certificada por el Consejo Internacional?

Una consultora en lactancia certificada por el Consejo Internacional (International Board Certified Lactation Consultant, IBCLC) es una proveedora de atención para la salud que cuenta con conocimientos y habilidades especiales para el manejo de la lactancia. Para convertirse en IBCLC, la persona debe aprobar un examen que aplica el Consejo Internacional de examinadores de consultoras de lactancia. Estas consultoras trabajan en hospitales, en las clínicas de WIC y en los consultorios de los proveedores de atención para la salud, así como en la práctica privada. La consultora en lactancia certificada por el Consejo Internacional puede darte confianza en tu capacidad de amamantar y ayudarte a resolver cualquier problema que pueda surgir.

Para encontrar a una consultora en lactancia certificada por el Consejo Internacional en tu área, comunícate con...

International Lactation Consultant Association
2501 Aerial Center Parkway, Suite 103
Morrisville, NC 27560
Tel: (888) 452-2478
Correo electrónico: info@ilca.org
Sitio web: ilca.org

¿Qué es una líder de la Liga de la Leche?

Una líder de la Liga de la Leche es una madre experimentada que ha amamantado a sus propios hijos durante por lo menos 1 año y ha recibido capacitación para responder tus preguntas acerca de la lactancia. Para convertirse en líder de la Liga de la Leche, la persona debe estar acreditada por la Liga Internacional de la Leche, una organización cuyo único fin es ayudar a las madres a amamantar. Las líderes de la Liga de la Leche son representantes de la Liga Internacional de la Leche y prestan sus servicios en forma voluntaria.

Para encontrar a una líder de la Liga de la Leche en tu área, comunícate con...

La Leche League International
P.O. Box 4079
Schaumburg, IL 60168-4079
Tel: (800) 525-3243
Sitio web: llli.org

¿Qué es una compañera consejera de lactancia?

La compañera consejera de lactancia es una madre que ha amamantado a sus propios hijos y que ayuda a otras madres de su comunidad a hacerlo. Para convertirse en compañera consejera de lactancia, la persona debe completar un programa de capacitación. Las compañeras consejeras de lactancia pueden trabajar como voluntarias o recibir pago de alguna agencia.

Para encontrar a una compañera consejera de lactancia en tu área, comunícate con tu hospital local, departamento de salud o clínica de WIC.

 Mamás y papás que comparten consejos acerca de la lactancia:
babygooroo.com/video/advice/sp

CAPÍTULO 9
EXTRAS

¿Qué significa esa palabra?

Alveolos: los alveolos son grupos de células que se encuentran en el interior del seno, y son las encargadas de producir la leche.

Areola: la areola es la parte más oscura del seno, alrededor del pezón.

Calostro: el calostro es la primera leche que producen los senos.

Reflejo de chorro de leche: cuando el seno libera la leche, esto se conoce como el reflejo de chorro de leche.

Conducto de leche: los conductos de leche son tubos pequeños que transportan la leche desde las células productoras (alveolos) hasta los orificios del pezón.

Glándula de Montgomery: las glándulas de Montgomery son bultos pequeños en forma de espinillas que se encuentran en la parte más oscura del seno, alrededor del pezón (areola).

Registro diario

Saca copias de esta página para mantener un registro diario durante las primeras 2 a 4 semanas.

DÍA	ALIMENTACIONES 8 A 12	PAÑALES MOJADOS 6 A 8	PAÑALES SUCIOS 3 A 4
EJEMPLO	JHT JHT I	JHT I	IIII
LUNES			
MARTES			
MIÉRCOLES			
JUEVES			
VIERNES			
SÁBADO			
DOMINGO			

Acerca de la autora

Amy Spangler, MN, RN, IBCLC, es esposa, madre, enfermera, consultora en lactancia, educadora y autora. Obtuvo su licenciatura en enfermería en la Universidad Estatal de Ohio (Ohio State University) y su maestría en salud materna e infantil en la Universidad de Florida (University of Florida). Amy es enfermera registrada y consultora en lactancia certificada por el Consejo Internacional (International Board Certified Lactation Consultant); fue presidente de la Asociación Internacional de Consultoras de Lactancia (International Lactation Consultant Association) y directora del Comité para la Lactancia de los Estados Unidos (United States Breastfeeding Committee). Amy ha trabajado con madres, bebés y familias durante más de 30 años. Ella y su esposo viven en Atlanta, Georgia, y tienen dos hijos.

baby gooroo

Para obtener más información
acerca de nuestros productos,
comunícate con:

baby gooroo
P.O. Box 501046
Atlanta, GA 31150-1046
Tel: (770) 913-9332
Fax: (770) 913-0822
Correo electrónico: info@babygooroo.com
Sitio web: babygooroo.com